A Fold In The River

... born of a folding
sketchbook, writer's
notebooks, drawings,
poems, walking and
a conversation with
each other's work ...

A Fold In The River

Philip Gross | Valerie Coffin Price

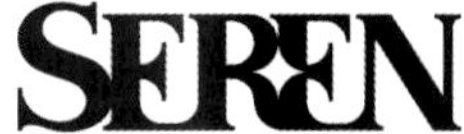

Seren is the book imprint of
Poetry Wales Press Ltd
Nolton Street, Bridgend, Wales

www.serenbooks.com
facebook.com/SerenBooks
Twitter: @SerenBooks

ISBN 978-1-78172-233-6

A CIP record for this title is available from the British Library

The publisher works with the financial assistance of the Welsh Books Council

Printed by Akcent Media Ltd

Contents

The River Next Door

1. The garden comes down to the river…

… with drowned corn-dolls
of flood-wrack in the wire,
          our fiction of a border,
the last post up-torn,
          up-tangled, rammed back
at an angle in the grey silt
          with baroque scrunched lager cans,
one flip-flop, and a corrugated
          rust-fret fine as peeled bark,

while what's left of the fence
          drift-nets the stream
snagging quick shreds of blue
          cement bags slim as fish.
(There *are* fish, too, like sinewy
          dreams, head on and fighting
upstream home to Merthyr.)

2. *Water Table*

All summer it lazed
                    on its stone-bed – half
the autumn too. Rain barely stirs it. Only

up, under the hills,
                    in the dark long (centuries-
long) hall weight shifts, the water table

being laid: the not-
                    yet-woken guests'
cups fill, are filled, are running over. Then

the day. A meadhall
                    clamour. Rain sheets
off the fields, the glistening flanks. It spills

into present-time, smells
                    sour, knows no bounds,
remembers too much and will not be stilled.

3. *The house wants to go back…*

...to the river. It breathes
water up through its bones

in shadows, small bouquets
of salts, crisp-dusty on the plaster.

Windows grow weepy. Mortar,
wearied, with its lime leached out

by rising damp and time
reverts to stream-bed gravel

that trickles away, leaving nubs
of raw river-stone, blunt

from the hard knocks
of the flood beach, only roughly settled:

an accommodation
to each other and to gravity

we call a house.
Where its corset of render has buckled,

it's been patched and cracks again.
Tap here or here, or here, a hollowness

responds – blown resonating spaces
like a Greek mask, an appalled

or gurning jar-head, face
to the amphitheatre's empty rows,

much as we address the far slope,
Cefn Glas with that velvety green

of a written-out slag heap –
the mute knowledge how one nearby

hillside changed one day
losing its grip, dissolving inwardly

(a long-buried spring and one too many
days of rain) as it let itself go

like a black sigh, coal-slurry and grit-sludge,
only wanting to be river

but there was a village in the way.

4. *A coal pebble*

: greyish, with a slight glint at one angle, not quite
stone, but oval and wafery, light to the touch.
(Skimmed low, it could walk on the water
almost, right up to that panicky
teeter at the end.)

It comes clean as any other from the river, as if
innocent – bland, black and innocent – of what it did.
What it left. (Not just under the hills
here but under the valley,
the Deep Navigation

past saving, sealed, filling with emptiness, drip
by rising drip like a glass harp (séance music,
its inhuman purity of tone). A cave-diver
might yet stoop and crawl
through the long sump

dragging his budget of air behind him, half
astronaut, half miner of that worked-out near-
unreachable inner space, peering
into the night of the male
soul, a lamp in his hat.)

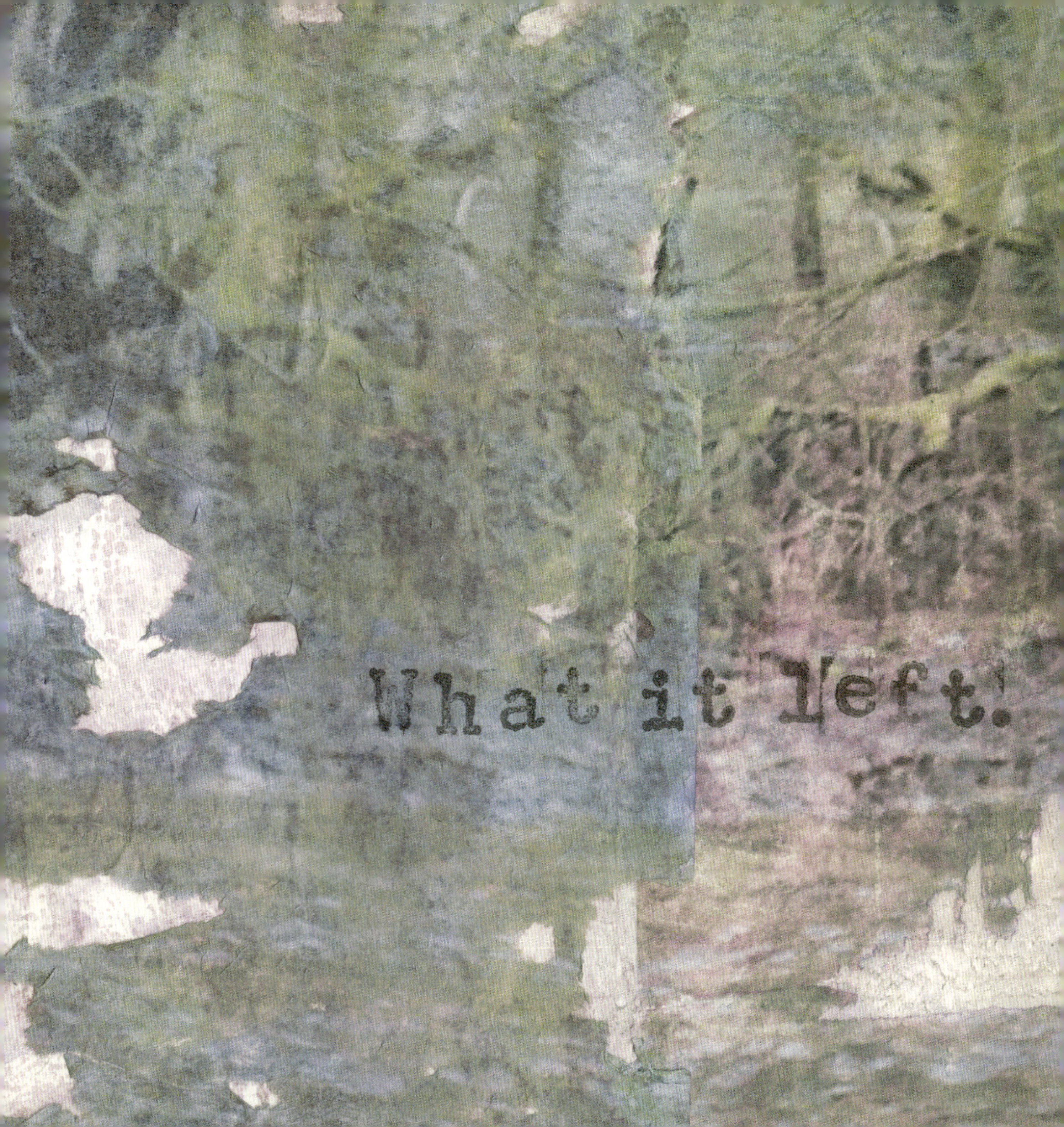
What it left!

...the Deep

past saving, sealed, filling wi
by rising drip like a glass ha

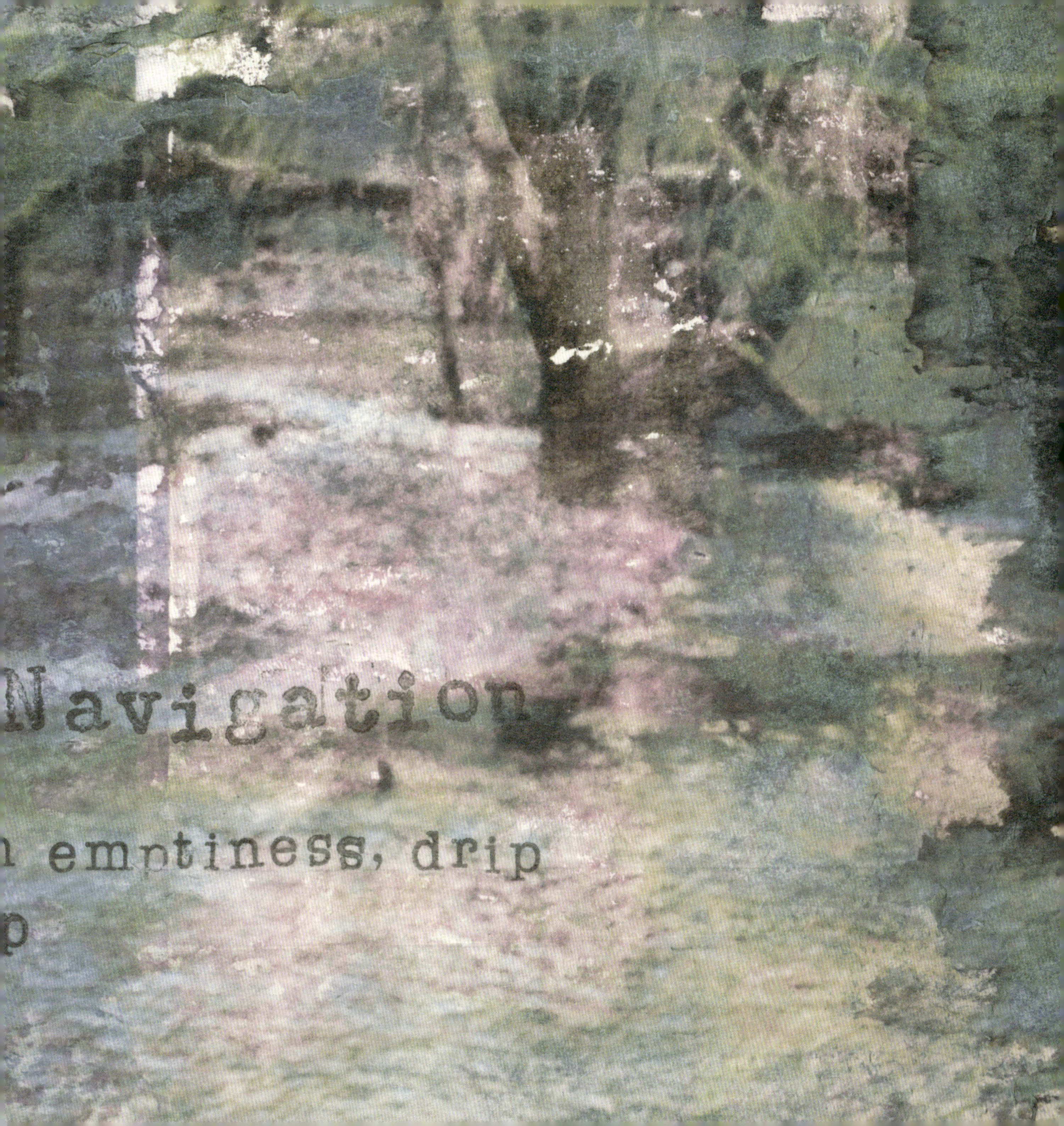
Navigation
emptiness, drip
p

5. *What's to do with it*

: that old muscle and wit
with which the Taff rises? Mad
bad pranks, extreme japes, anything

(like the kids who torch the bracken
leaving slim birch saplings ashen-
white and shrivelled) just to make a mark...

I found three bicycles, a rust-contraption
wrangling in the shallows, twisted into one another
in a circus strongman's knot.

I lost count of the draggled buggies
that beached awhile, then bumped by
like a skeleton pram-push, jolt by nudge

for years, Quixotic, off
to blight the views of Cardiff Bay.
And the bikes? I waded in, all good intentions,

tugged and slipped and swore. Gave up
on recycling. Looked around, then
kicked them back

to what the river wanted. Waved them on their way.

6. *It's nothing personal...*

the damp of this land, the way it rises. Or
not *rises* – *finds its level.* The hills
are a column of water

that each autumn fills to the skyline. Each
slope of the valley is a green-
brown standing wave

like you see in a tide-rip, constant pressure,
isobars in tons per square inch,
the soil's weather.

What made you think you could live here
dryshod? (Or so says the soul-
surveyor. My full

report will follow in due course. And the bill.)

7. *A River Runs Through*

First, it was a boundary – in some sense
ours, our tape of un- and ever-changing
water music, our glitter-link fence…
Then it was up and sullen, disarranging

the edges of things. It was camped on the lawn.
Hadn't we seen the rag and plastic tidewrack
in the lower branches? We had been warned
and we still let it into our life. Now it falls back:

poor put-upon thing, it was trying to wash
itself clean, its tired towns, bringing nearly-new
hand-me-downs down like a gift, making lace

from landfill tampax, wearing away, in its rush
to cope, its damaged banks, wearing what face
but our own? We are what it flows through.

Taff valley, Quakers Yard

... **AND SUDDENLY, FLOOD** – the river was a cat, a kitten – slightly feral – now suddenly today, a whiff of tiger.

I say this to Jeremy. He's been walking up the hill behind their house. The streams, he says, are *bristling*.

Just a weekend of rain begins it, but it must have been the weeks before that brought the hills to saturation point. Now, everything that falls sheets off, and there at the end of the garden is this... other thing. Brown thing, all muscles. Standing waves in it.

And 'the end of the garden' has moved. Some metres closer, and two metres higher, overnight. It's not the volume of this new Taff (squared or cubed, not doubled) but the speed – breath-catching, like a high-speed through-train when you're on the platform, well stood back behind the yellow line, but still...

The stone beach is gone. Whole fallen boughs heave and slalom on past. There's a constant rip-curl round the trunks of trees and trailing branches. It's not up the garden, not yet, but it's *its* choice, not ours – as if the fence had come down at the zoo but the animals hadn't noticed, hadn't noticed *you*, not yet.

The Stain

It spreads – one touch
of water, and the ink
lets go –
as if the paper wants this, physically.
It bleeds
like damp through plaster,
as a worry-dream
you can't
recall persists, a smudge-print on the day.
It stays
like flood risk, like the once
in a hundred years
that (always)
could be this year, shadow on your title deeds –
coal stain
on the hearth or heart
that nothing shifts,
not suds or scrubbing,
risings of the river, year in year out, rinsings
of the rain...

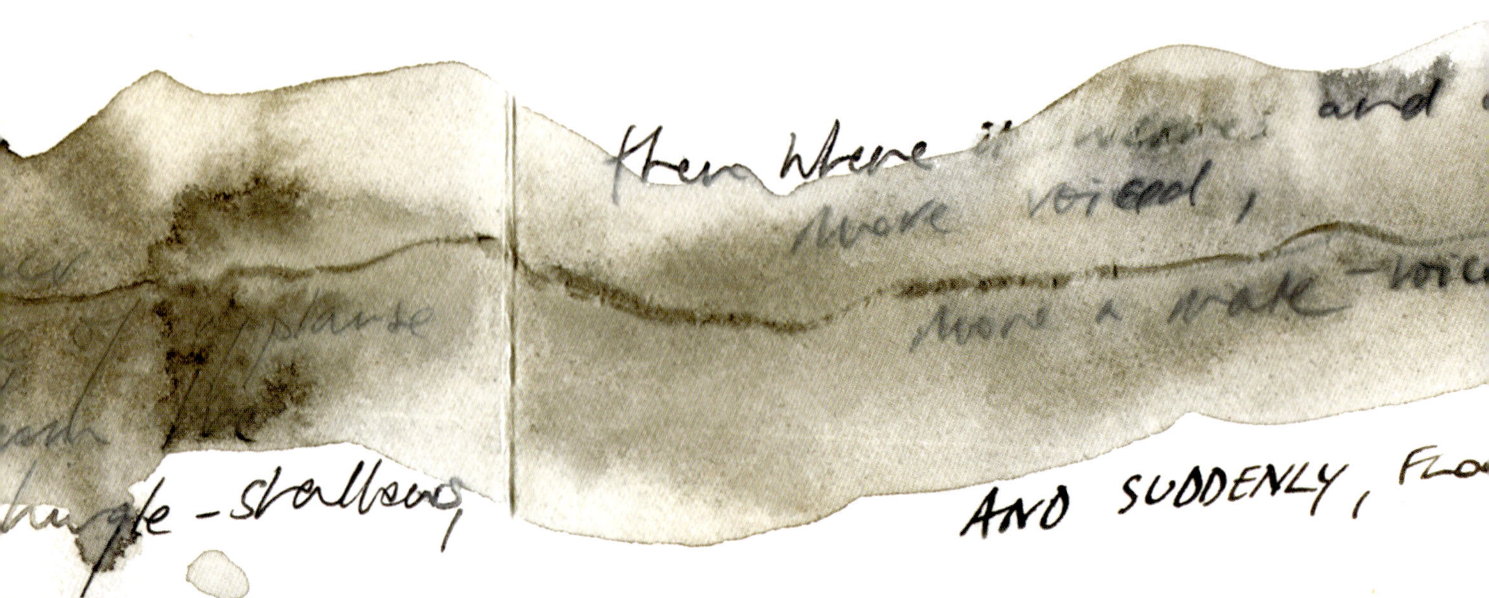

A river runs
through time
as well as space,

-epens,

-chair.

But soft- mutated too.

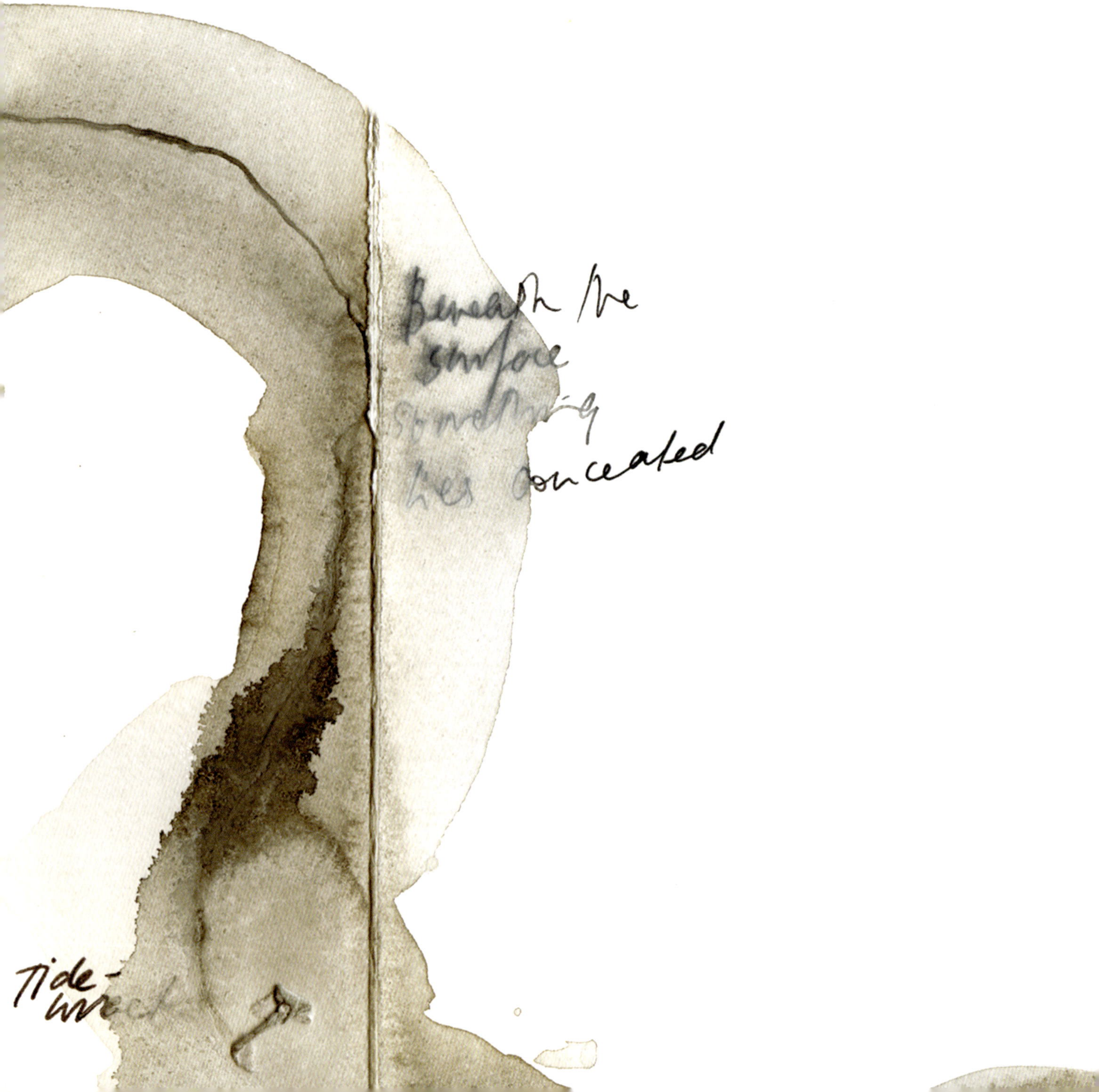

Beneath the
surface
something
lies concealed

Tide-
wrack

Folding The River

Don't tell me that it can't be done: to fold
the river. I've heard it, on the nearly edge of night

– suddenly loud, between narrowing sides
of itself, then shut. As a book. Mum. No

more stories tonight, children. Even, now

and then, in daylight, you blink: the river
concertinas, thirty miles from source to swerve

to sump to sluice gate, glint to shadow,
past to present, like a secret we're all in on –

we're all in. What could open a wide enough gaze

to read us, but a river? Or this: *orihon*...
On mulberry paper as fine as closed eyelids,

in ink made of soot and glue, the nested scroll
could open this way, that or both, each unknown

to the other. Or could leave it sleeping, fold on fold.

orihon : traditional Japanese folding book

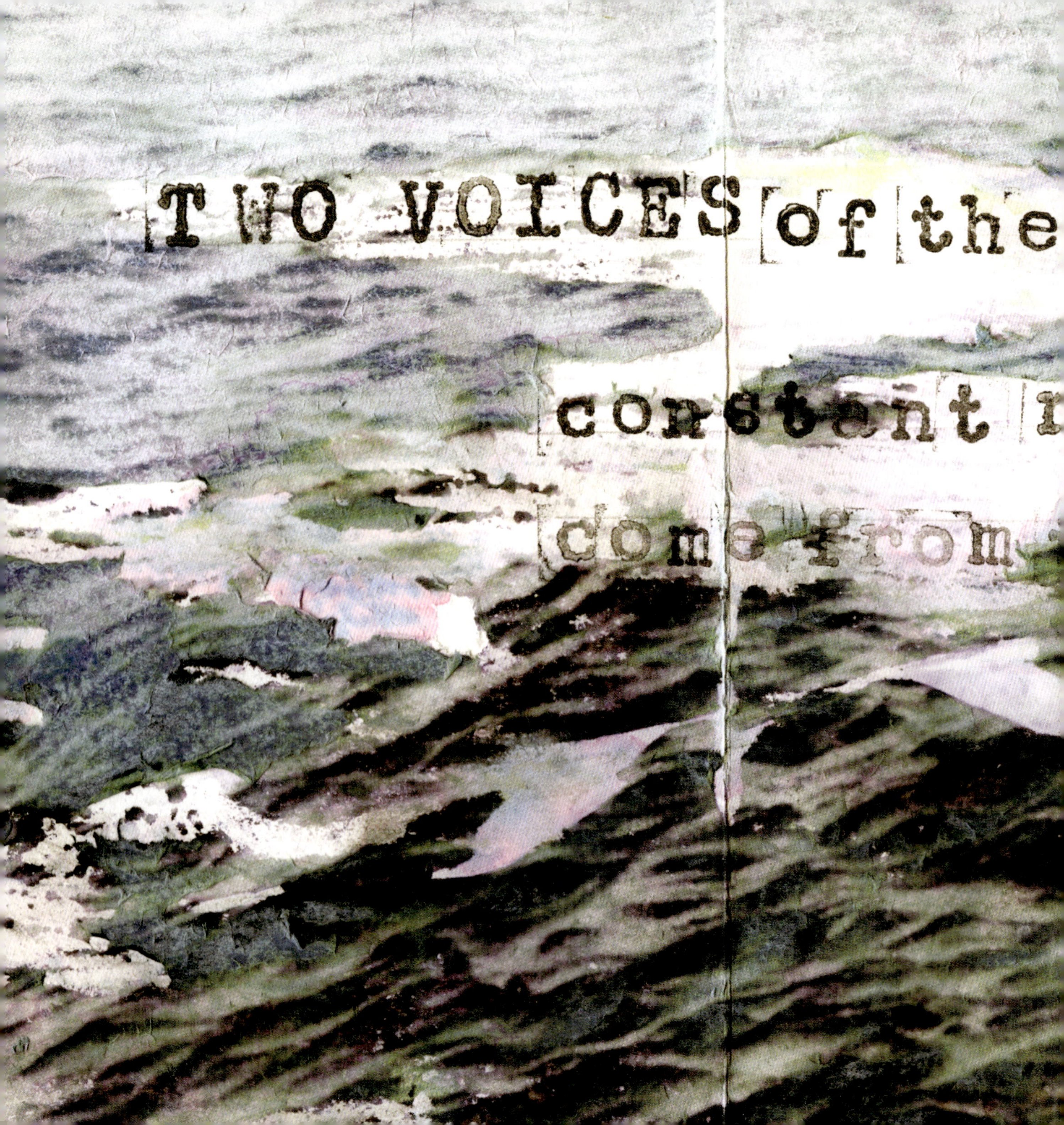
TWO VOICES of the
constant
come from

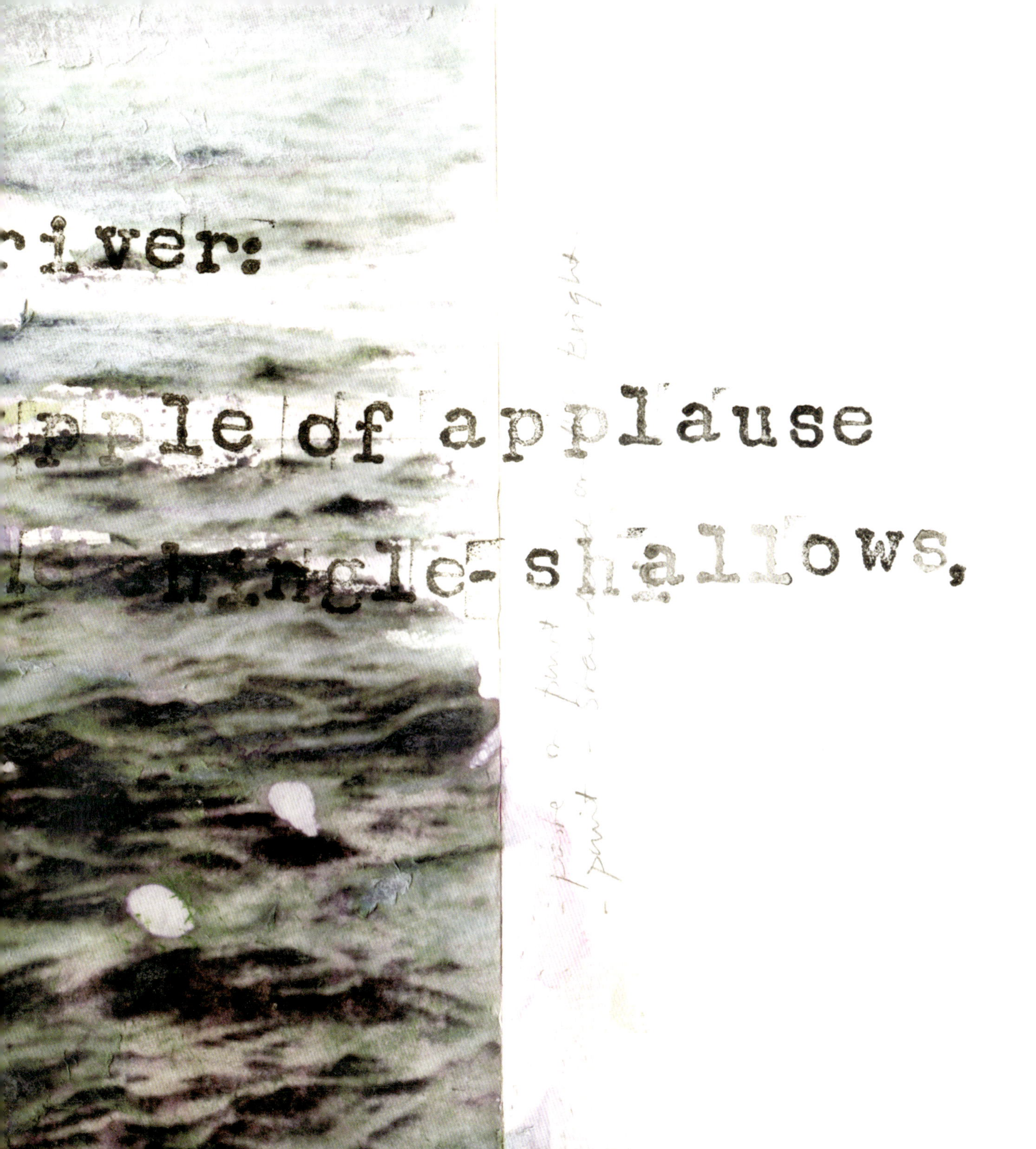
river:
pple of applause
shingle-shallows,

... **FLOOD BEACH** with a morning after face.
River back in its own bed, innocent
          but for draggles of fly-by-night beach grass
          laid flat, some new pools,

a dank look in surprising places,
tall balsam up by the roots.
          Goings-on after dark, such hasty
          tidyings away. That guilty look.

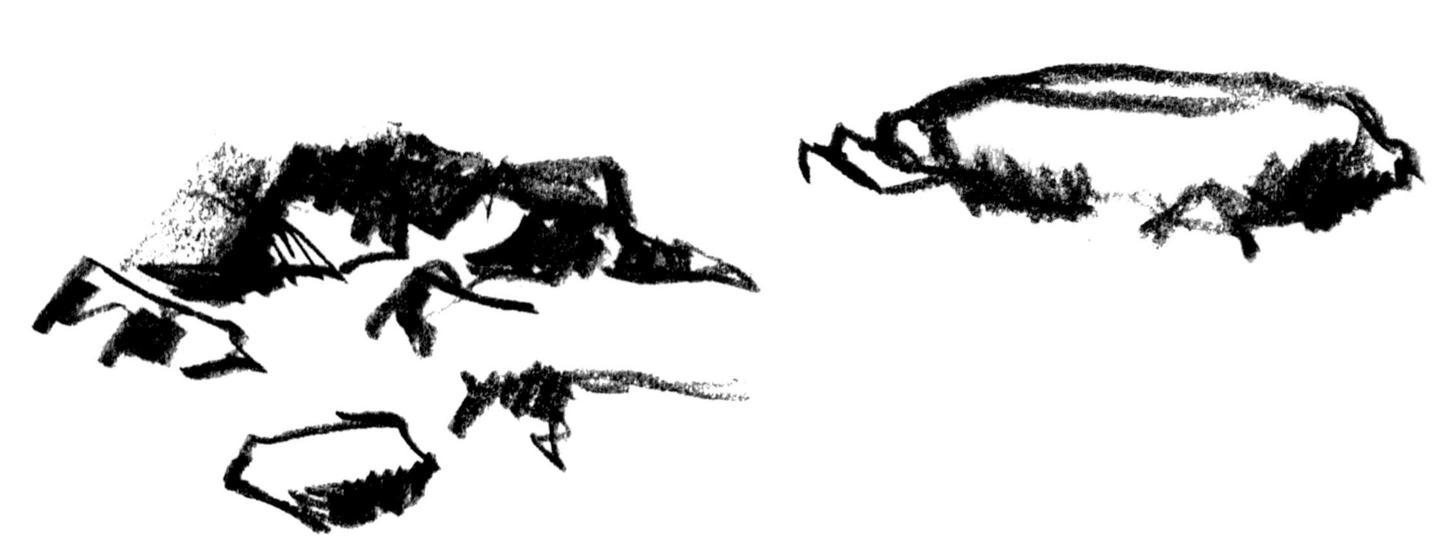

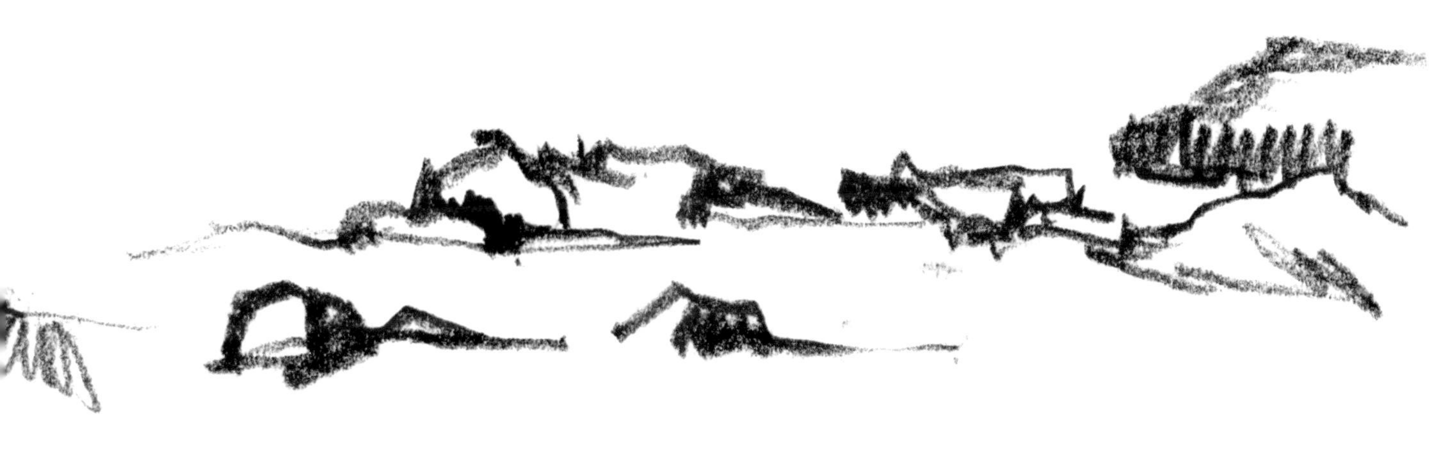

... **TWO VOICES** of the river: constant ripple of applause come from the shingle-shallows, then where it swerves and deepens, more *voiced*, more a male-voice-choir. But soft-mutated too.

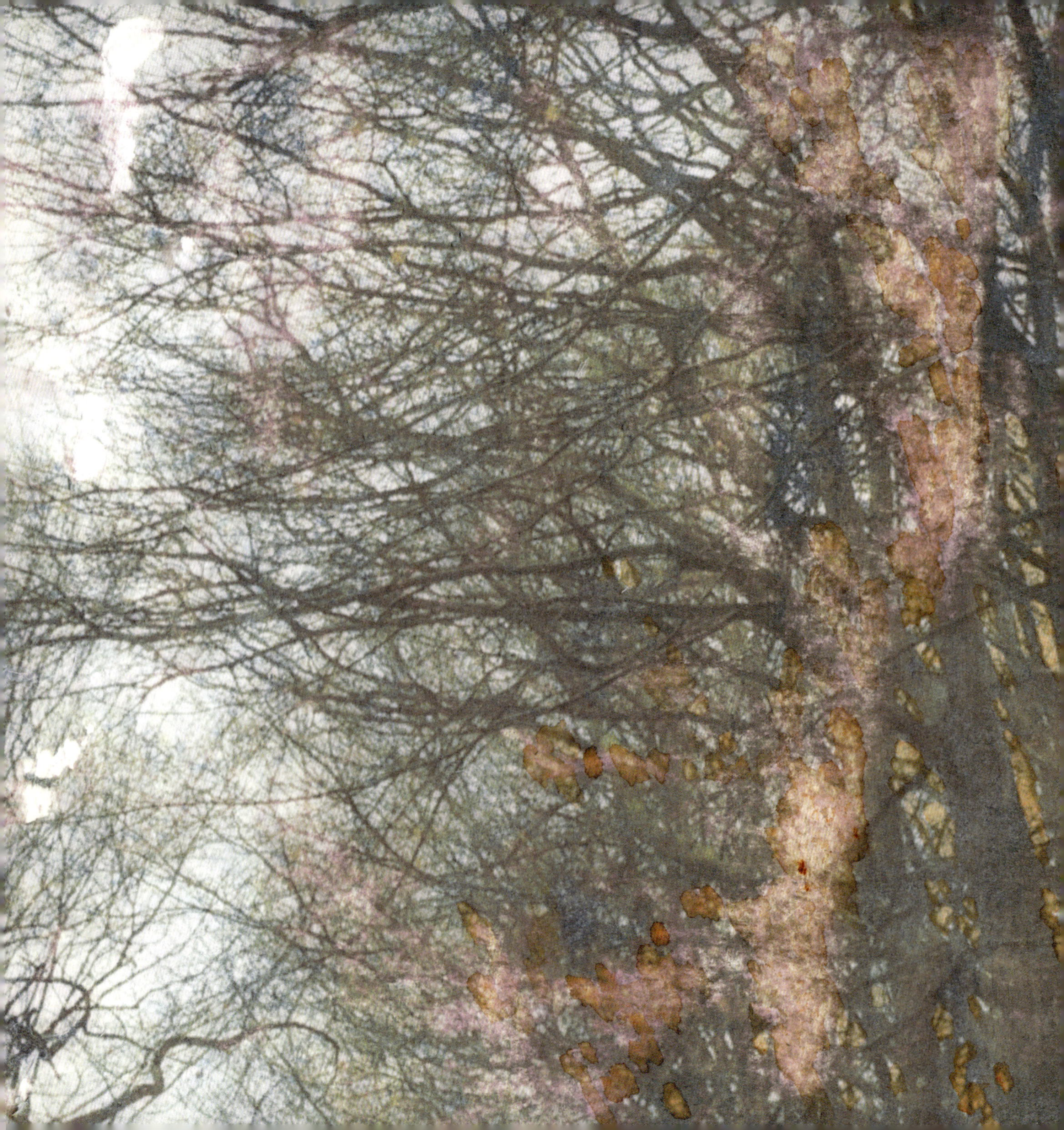

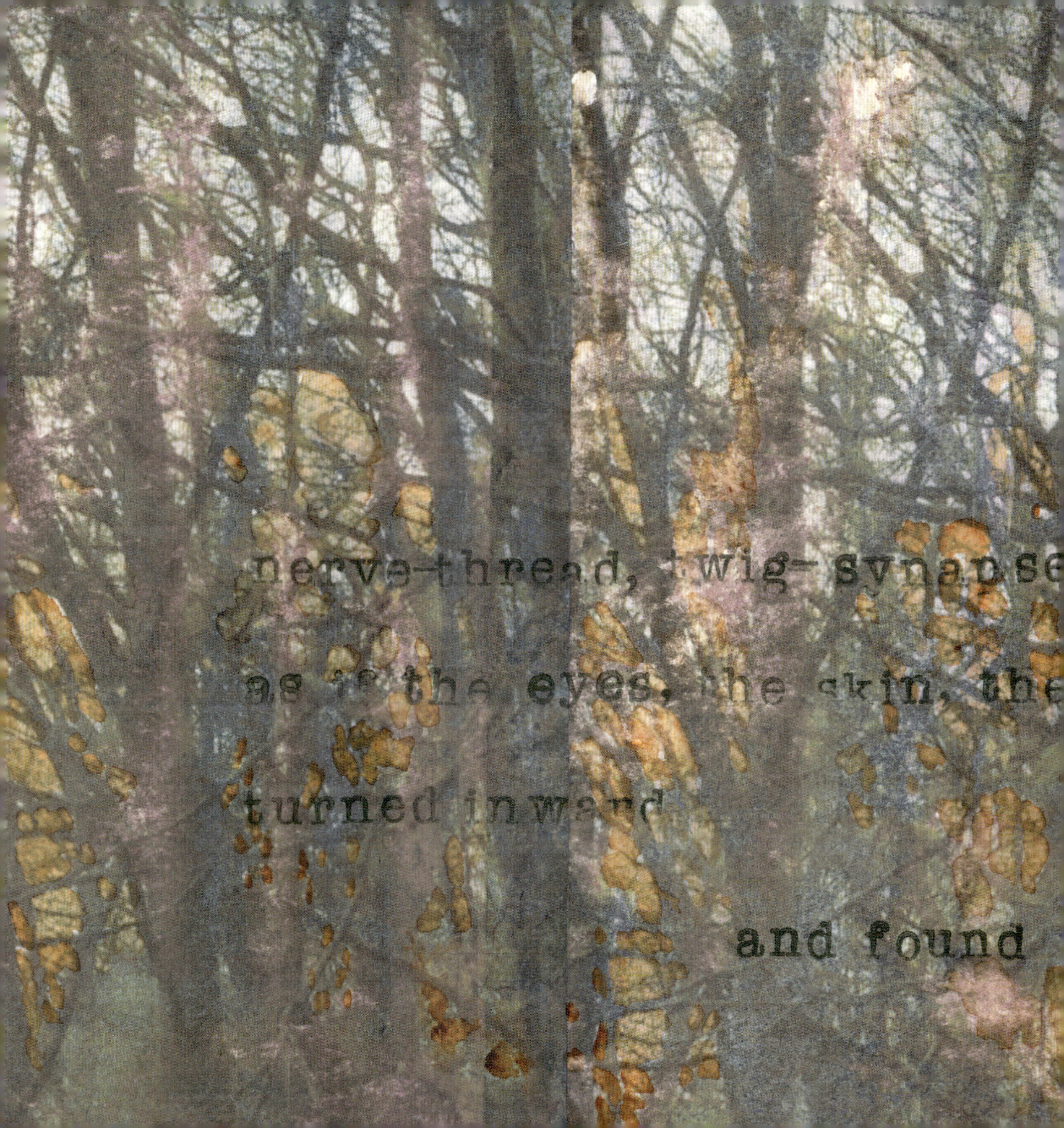

nerve-thread, twig-synapse

as if the eyes, the skin, the

turned inward

and found

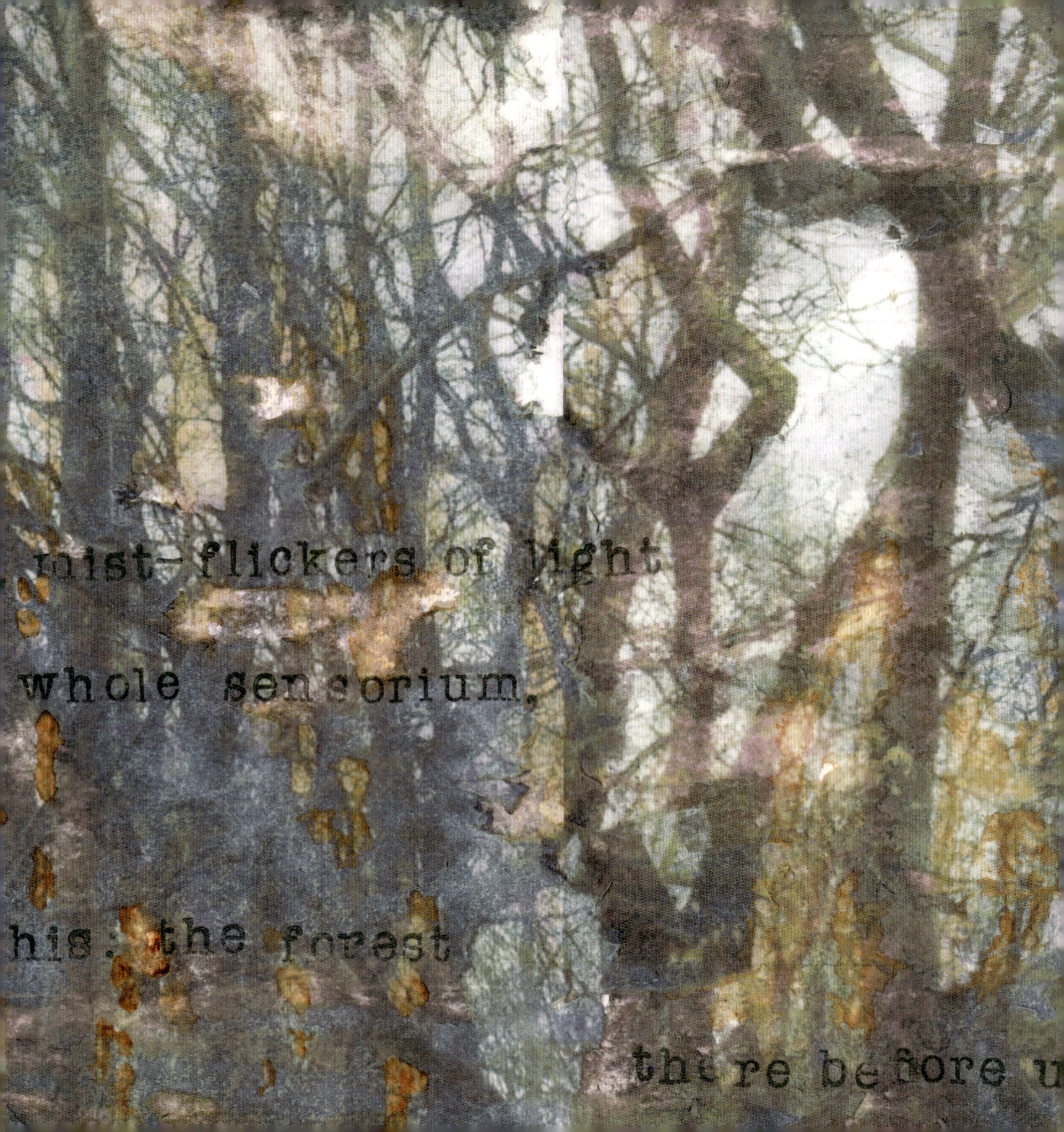

mist-flickers of light

whole sensorium,

his: the forest

there before u

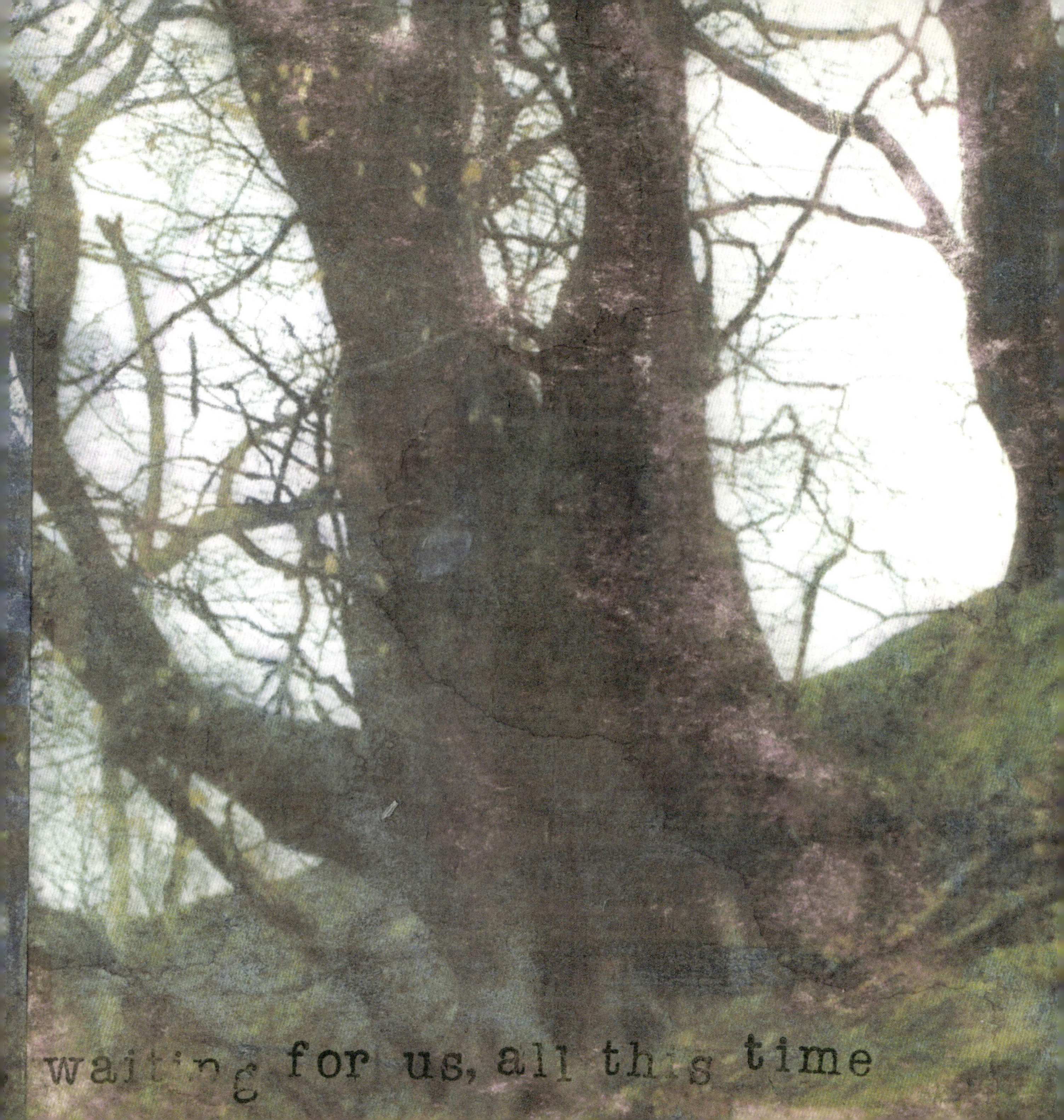
waiting for us, all this time

Fire In The River

Between two flows: the down-
pour of the bonfire's uprush and the river's
crackling over stone and stone and stone

(neither with any thought of stasis –
if they so much as entertained it, then
what would they be?) ... a stillness. See

us from the farther bank, our flames held
steady in reflection, as if underwater,
like the rippling absence in the heart

of fire. We're burning knotweed, spit-
and-wheezing from its hollow stalks,
insatiable; we're burning flood-wrack

as a night mist fills the valley,
round a tepee of twigs held briefly
by the flare-up that would pull it in,

the house of fire. The thrust of it
straight upwards in motionless air.
Above us, here and nowhere

else, a clearing – as if our slight
disturbance of each mist-molecule's
poise was enough to tip the balance…

The sky's eye opening on us. See us
small and smaller still, from out there. Space
beyond amazement. Its unsparing clarity.

Looking back now, from under the slick
and dark shuddery gloss
of the river – the eye

of a fire left to burn itself out.
It gathers in its glow,
yes, it knows

what it knows; is always almost
torn off, downstream,
but snagged on a twig,

a mere circumstance, already
tattering; is held
more by your gaze

than anything its own. A fire
sunk, that consumes
itself in recollection,

shrunk from the day-and-night
glare over Dowlais
sealed over with smoke.

An immense dark heap of cinders...
Only when the shades of night
have settled... the fire within

manifests itself. The water tries
to suck it under,
but it won't let go.

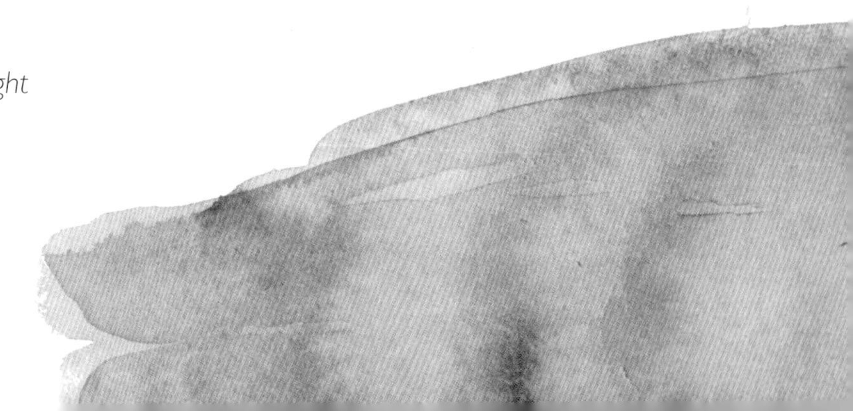

... TWILIGHT, EARLY JUNE – a grey-green satiny touch to the light over the water, under the big beech – reflected sky only there, in midstream, none overhead from here – smooth light, heavier and slower, so it feels, than running water,

and now a splash, a flaw in the surface (only the effects of light and shadow make it visible – reflection gives us what the eye can't see direct) – my eyes, struggling (at my age) between light and dark, for focus – and yes, there are blurs, it's not me: little quick faint blurs of light – as I sit on the stone now still enough to see their tracks, low swerving runs across the darker pools, the insect places – moths?

but with a purpose: bats! – *[later, a knowledgeable friend says 'Daubentons' and 'they live up in the abandoned railway tunnel' but for now they're just that exclamation mark, hardly a word attached]* – so-close-skimming the water their wing tips leave pocks in the surface, and so fast I don't see – or not them, only a pale-fawn see-through blur – like subatomic particles, a statistical probability of bats – nothing so crude as mere existence...

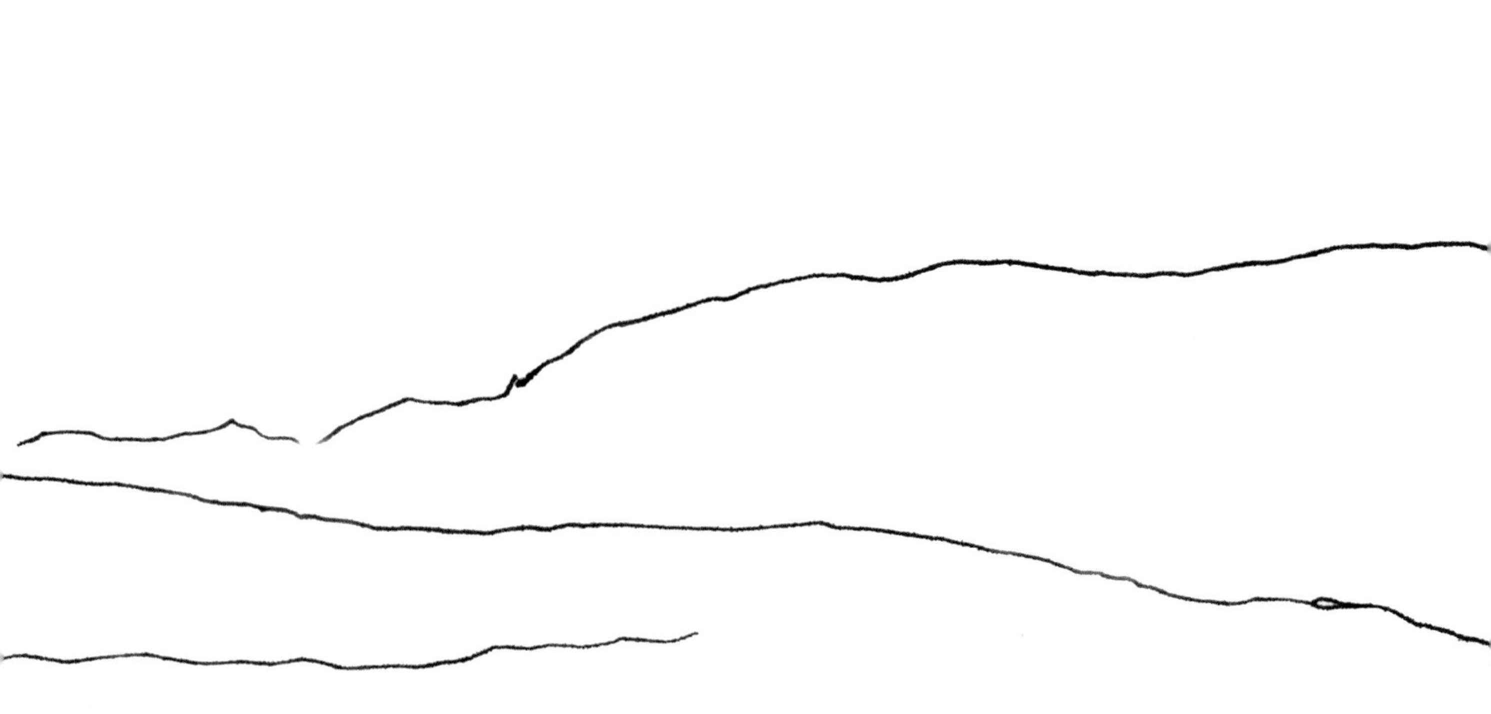

... **GROUND** – what counts as ground in these valleys? Nothing absolute – an equation with water and time. That skyline, Craig yr Efail, with a small hanger of trees, askew, a feather in its cap – climb there and you realise you've just reached ground level, a plateau incised by rivers.

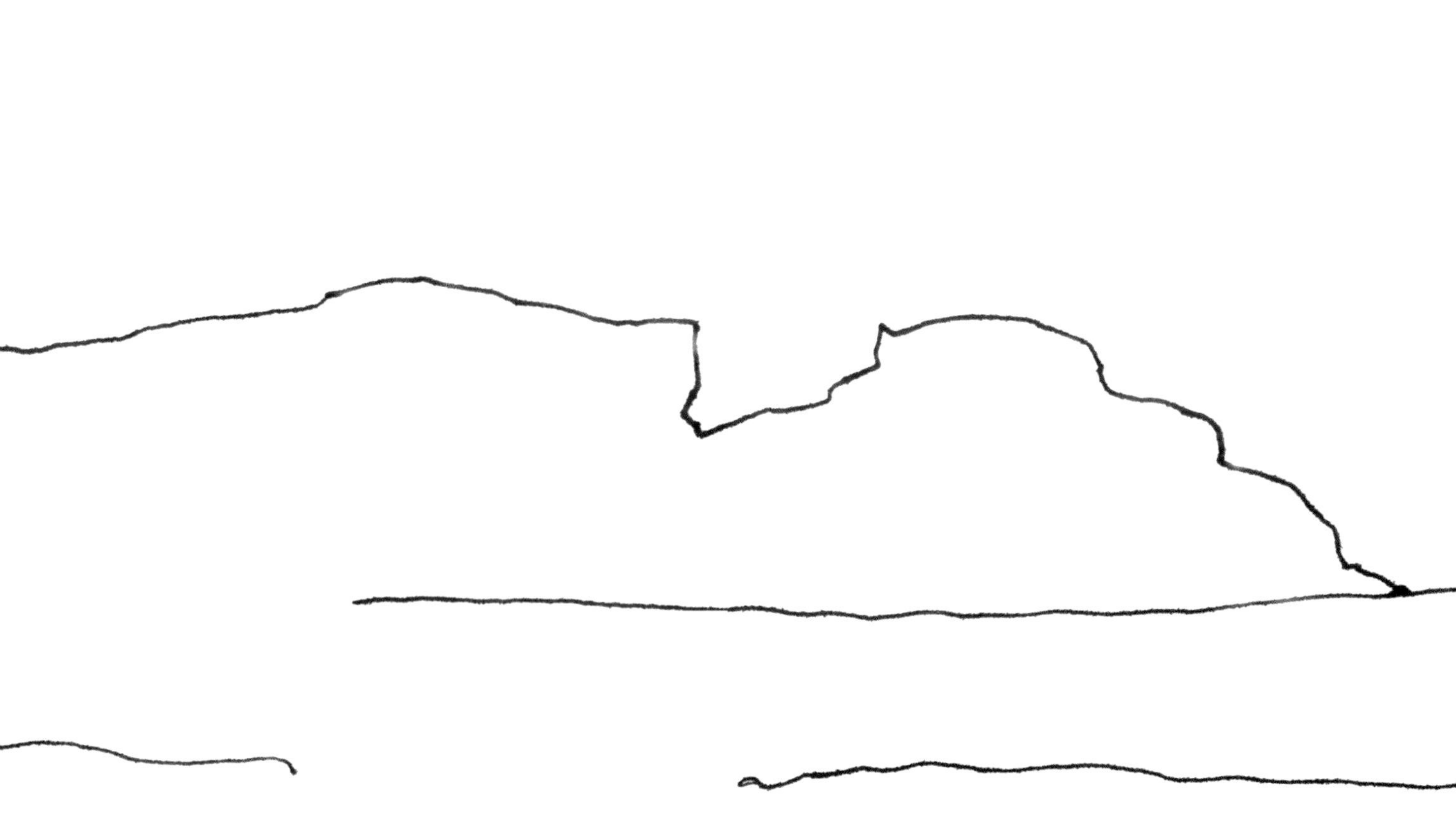

Mornings when the mist fills the valley to the brim, you're looking across the uncut landscape, before water carved its habits in. Now you climb down through the strata (exposed here and there, in outcrops or pockmarks of quarries) – you could fear that you're burying yourself. Or feel contained, arrived, like coming home.

Scar

: a heart-
shaped scorch-
patch in the bracken.
Today a spat of Valleys rain has stopped it there

but each Easter makes tinder of this hillside,
a swathe of crisp brown question-marks,
fire in them itching to run where it will

and how could you resist it, being fourteen
and full of the slack of the day, of the nothing
to go home to, with a lighter in your jeans,

the others looking on? A fair wind, luck,
and there'll be sirens this evening, smoke-
signalling *We were (are still) here*

where they'll already be too late,
those flatfoots in vizors and fire suits,
cartoon spacemen in the wrong film. Watch

them chasing the last of the flame-snakes,
wriggling here, there. Different greynesses
into the night sky: smoke and steam.

That's a good day, when everyone wakes
to sodden rakings-over, world restored
to black-and-white, shoots shrivelled

to wisps, bared rocks and birch trunks
scorched, a stink as alkaline as birdlime,
valley like a morning-after ashtray

(yes, you in the dinky estate by the station,
we'll rub your noses in it), like a riddled grate
of clinker, where coal was. Not far

beneath the skin of new-turfed green,
                    dug under but still
                              smouldering, the
                                        heart. The scar.

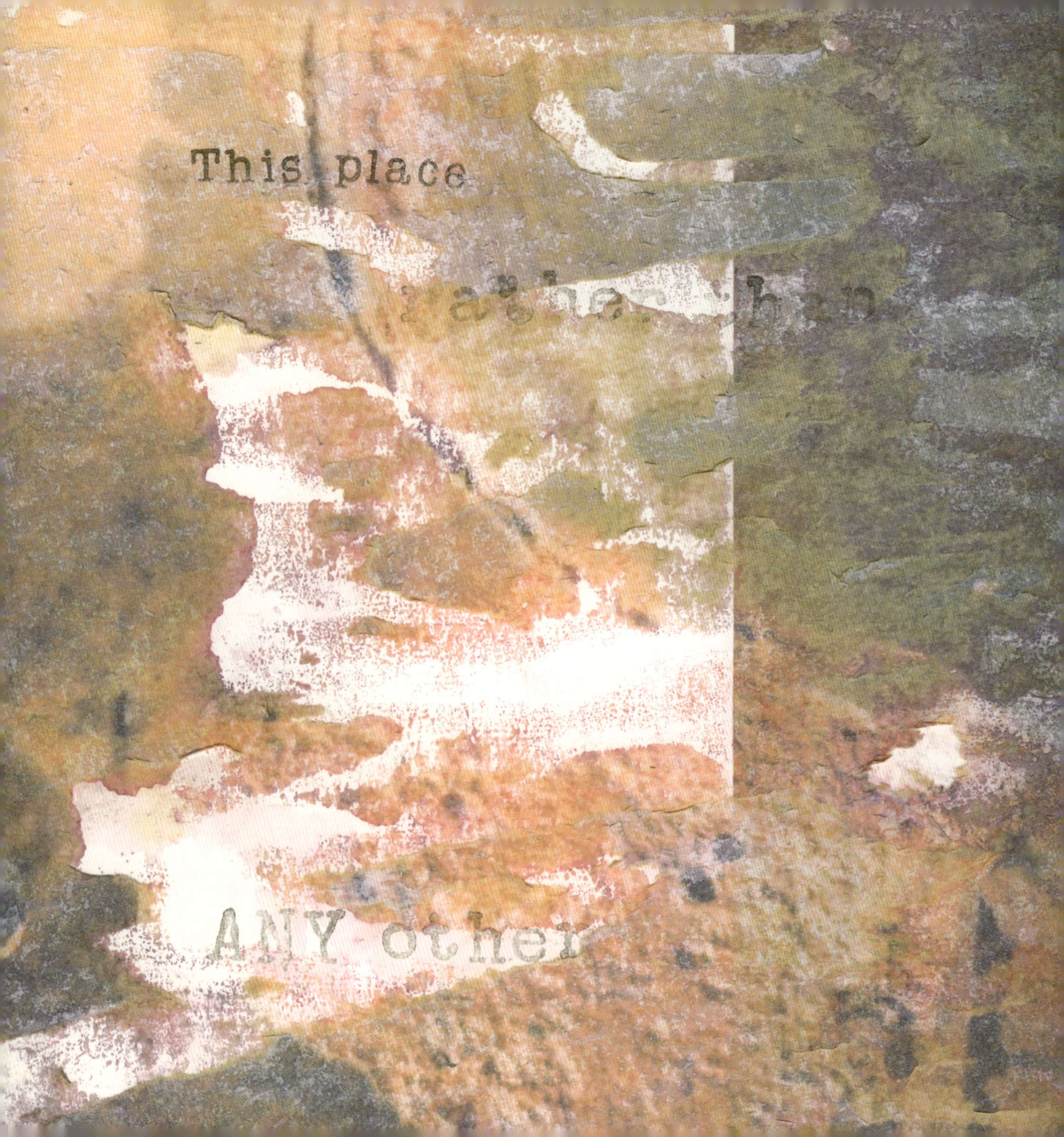

This place

rather than

ANY other

NOBODY

rather than any other

brambles

WAITING

... **SQUARE GROTTO**, like a holy well. This is downstream, on a rough path through the brambles, though it seems to follow a track, an old one, just above the river. In a little rock face, there's this low opening, almost as deep as it's (waist-) high, and in it, moss-green, there's a natural stoup of water, filled by constant trickles from the walls. A horse-trough, or a holy well, or a spring, for use by people... though nobody seems to come here, except whatever kids have left a folding bed and foam mattress burnt out just below. That, and an old bath mat draped on a low branch like a waiting leopard. So maybe something about this place does bring them here, of all slight clearings in the tangled woods, here rather than any other? I wonder if they know or notice what that something is?

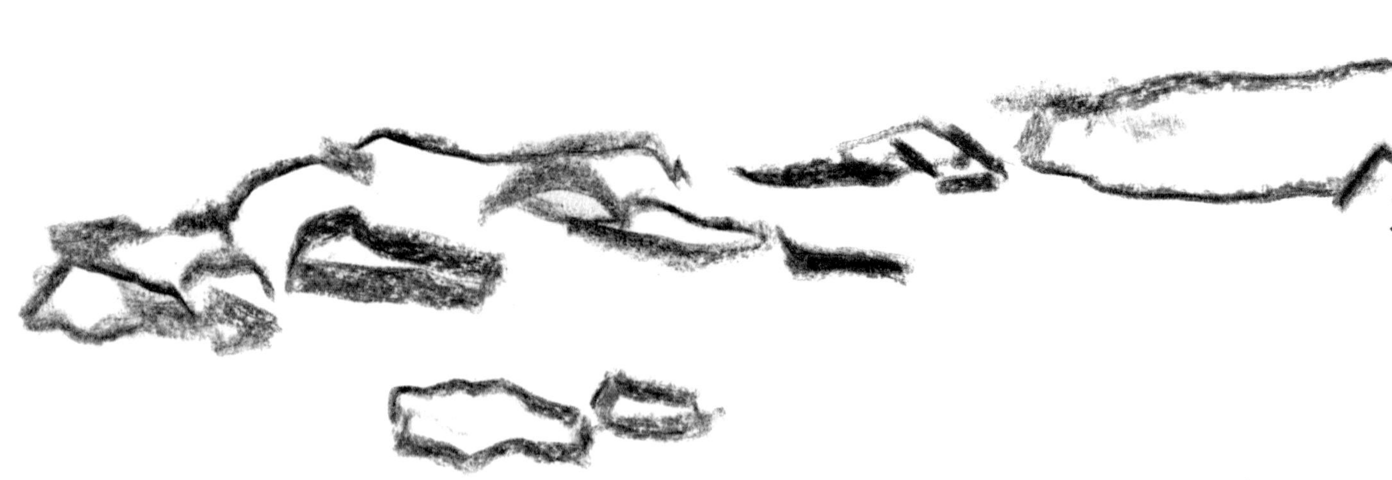

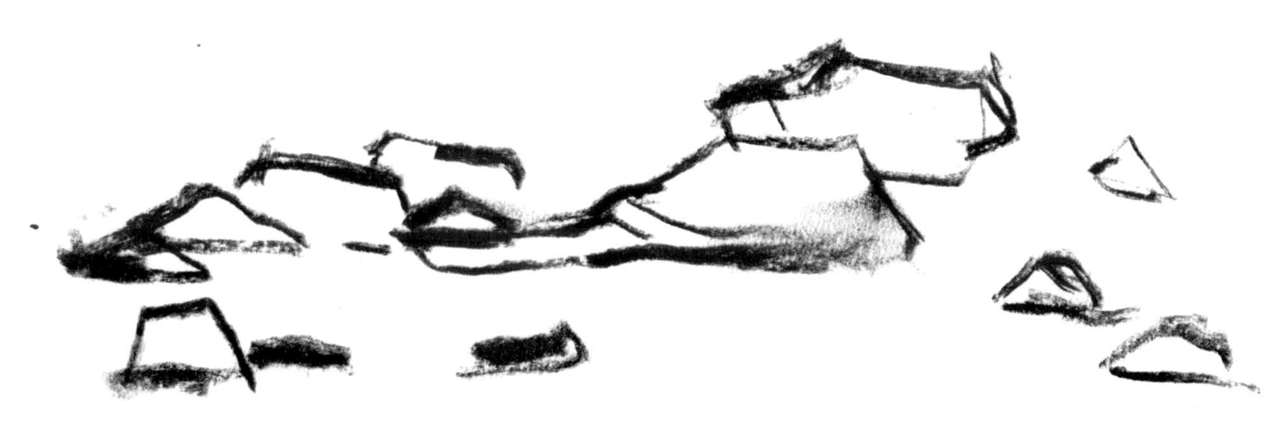

... **IN THE SHALLOWS**, a flicker of fry – in the khaki-clear slack-water under the far bank, sheltered by a spit of shingle – under the shade of a fallen, self-uprooted tree – quick and dark but nearly-transparent fishlings, visible only by their movement – no shoal but a hither-and-thither, short darts, skitter-scatter, back-doublings, off at angles, all a pattern that's no pattern, to confuse the predator's gaze.

Five Takes on the Taff

The river is
a tree that grows inwards
from the tips of its twigs,
sap reaching downhill until accidentally
it finds itself, its others;
finds itself a trunk, a place
to stand, this thing that can't
stand still; finds
a foot on the ground,
at last, that turns out
to be sea.

The river sits
down in the valley bottom, wide
skirts, many petticoats
of catchment round her,
rumpled up. Poor thing,
she takes it all to heart.

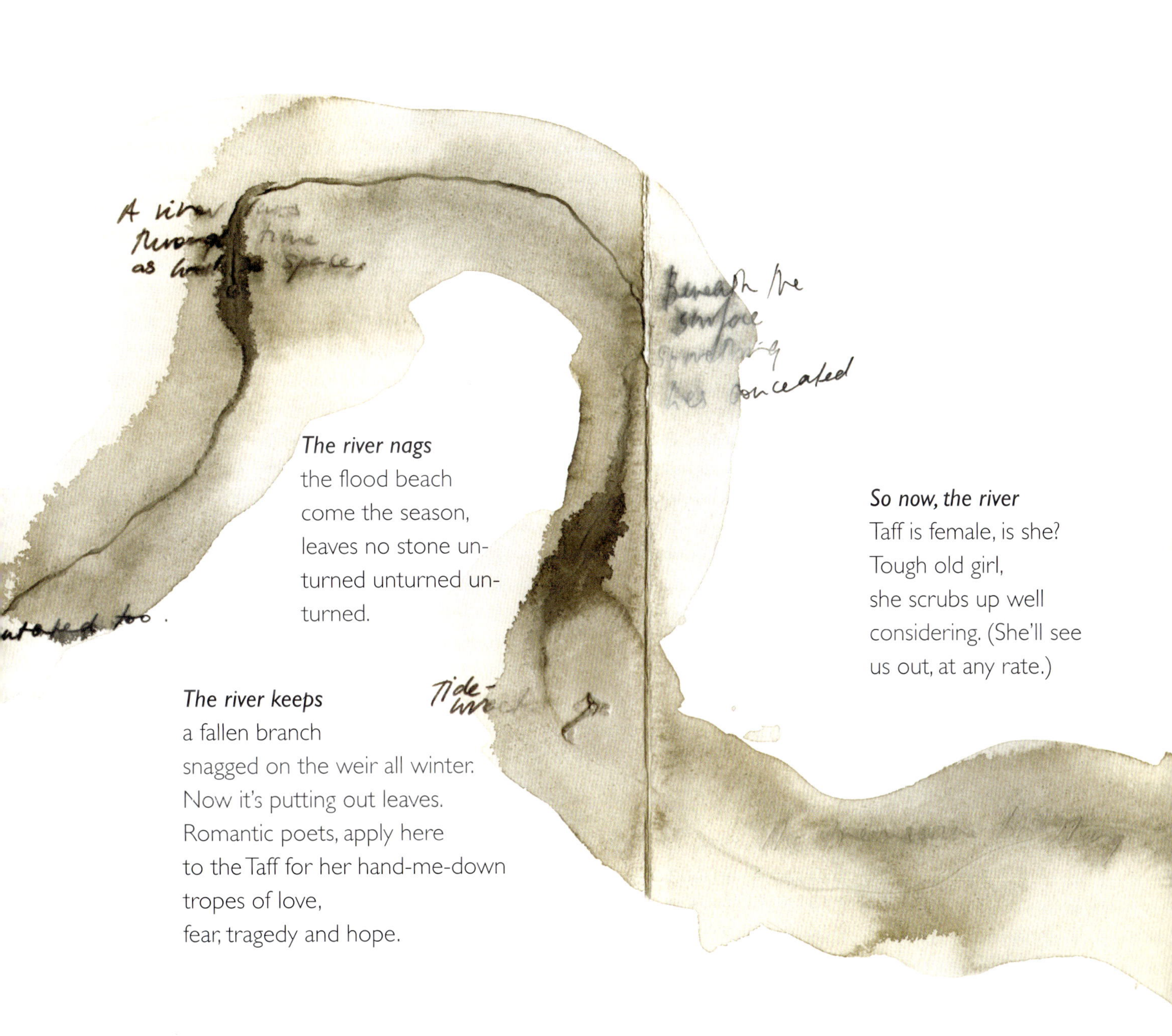

The river nags
the flood beach
come the season,
leaves no stone un-
turned unturned un-
turned.

The river keeps
a fallen branch
snagged on the weir all winter.
Now it's putting out leaves.
Romantic poets, apply here
to the Taff for her hand-me-down
tropes of love,
fear, tragedy and hope.

So now, the river
Taff is female, is she?
Tough old girl,
she scrubs up well
considering. (She'll see
us out, at any rate.)

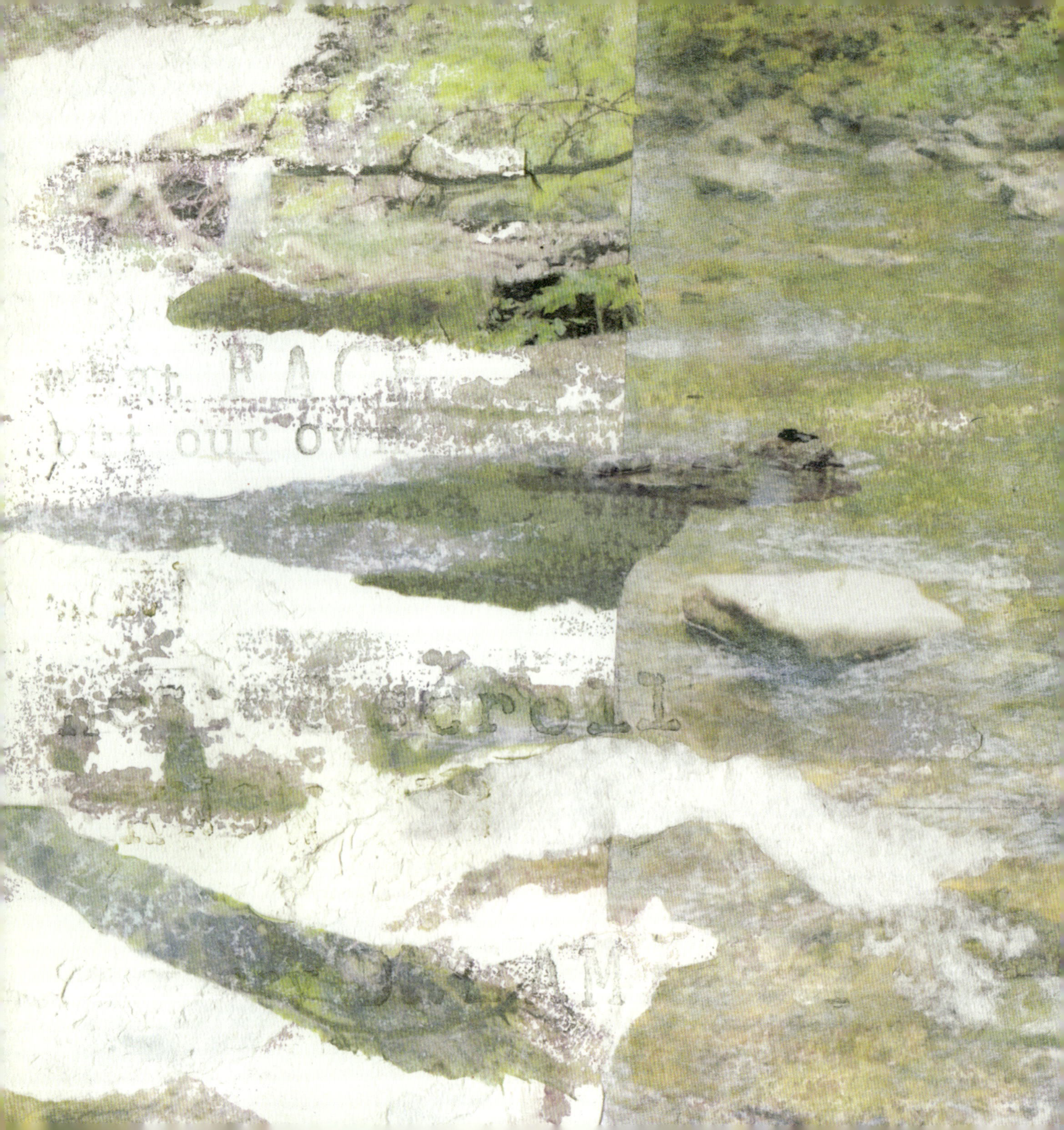

FAC
our ow
scroll

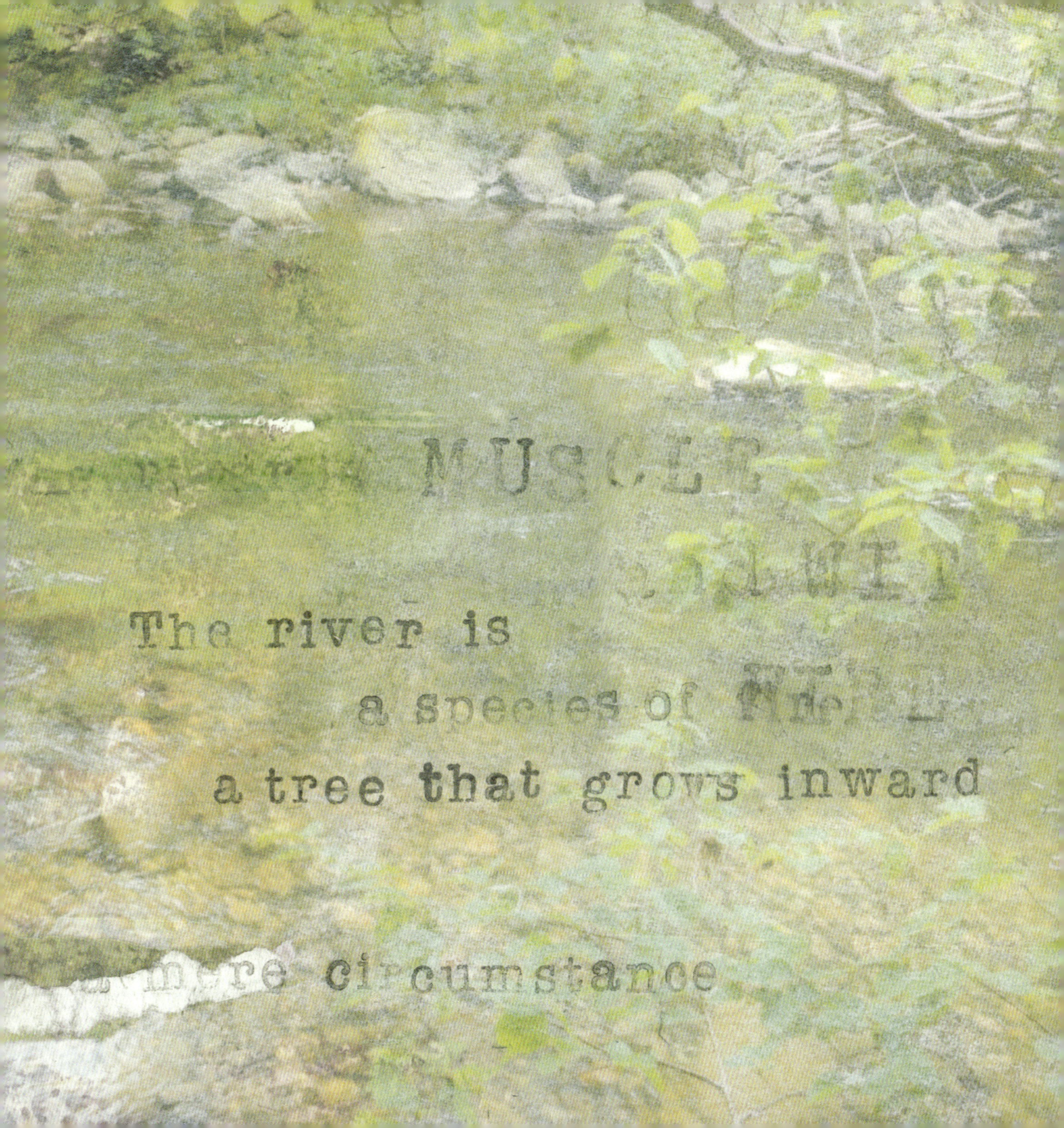
MUSCLE
The river is
a species of
a tree that grows inward
circumstance

... **BROKEN ARCHES**: two viaducts, demolished, in a wooded hillside, flying-buttresses with nothing to support. (A heavy load.) A gesture of parting, the kind that never leaves, that you can't quite forget. Not a folly, but relics, certainly – Roman / Romantic: *eheu*, *alas*, the lost *imperium* of coal and steam. Later generations saw the ruins on Aquae Sulis as the work of giants. We know it was founded on the blood and bones of slaves.

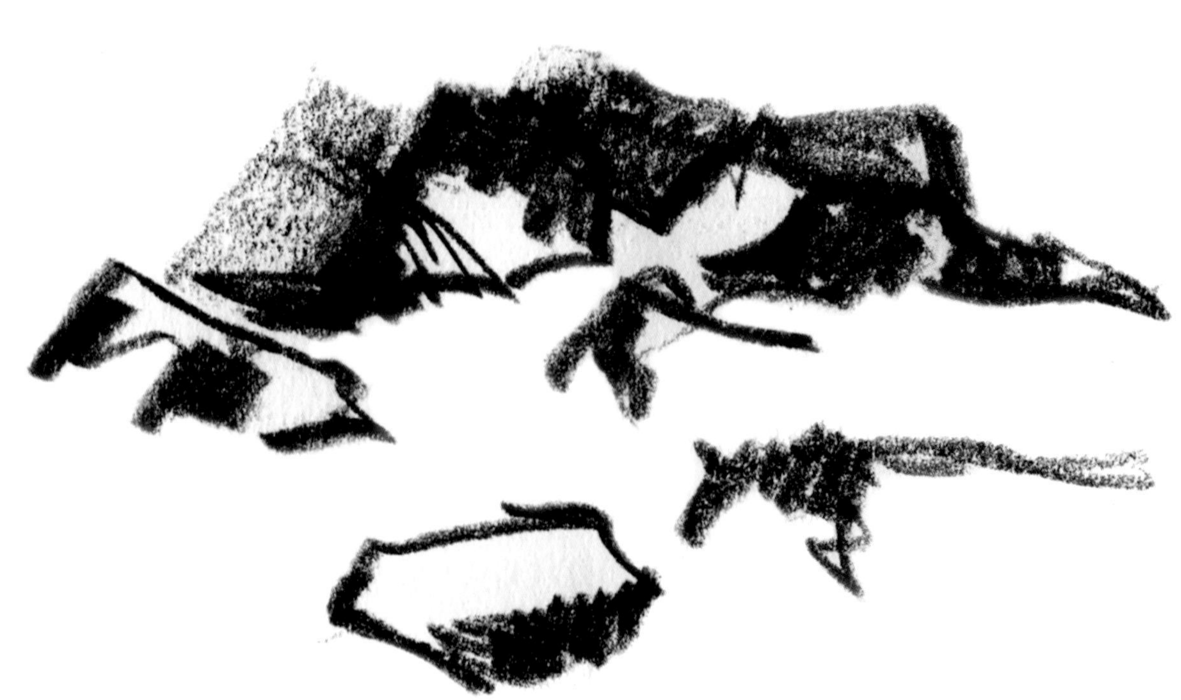

... **BRIEF AND MARGINAL** land of a flood beach, no visible soil. The scoured stones say it all: quick river, uppity, wham-bam and off, no silt-idling here. And yet all this grows:

balsam, naturally, a new kid on the blocks, on the stones – pink root-clumps casting round to find a purchase – so easily snapped, a stalk is just a column of crisp water, scented for temptation, also

soapwort and willowherb – mainly, though, the life is keeping low – with spreading creep-stems, starfish-fashion from each fortuitous root – for preference, between stones, not over, no profile at all,

tiny spikes of white petals, frost-green mat of silverweed that lays itself across the stones – here and there, blatant chancers: a potato or tomato there, or could be cousin Nightshade,

something big-leafed as a sunflower, straight up with nowhere to go – garden break-outs, convicts, transports with new lives in Botany Bay,

the outback, the wilderness-frontier we've gone half way round the world to find, though it's under our noses at home

… **CRESTING THAT SKYLINE**, first time: eye to eye across another valley with the tidemark of the sad estate – the top streets empty, windows blanked with perforated metal guards – sap sinking, the life draining down

... while here, on top, on levelled slag, the mountain flora: tight madder-red almost leafless plants like hill-coral – slim thistles lucent in the low sun – bird's-foot trefoil and tormentil: cloth of gold

... **STORM**. Broken branches, one across the tramway – half-rotten twigs have been stamped into bits.

Let's not rehearse the platitudes of autumn. Just remember: it is *meant* to break things down.

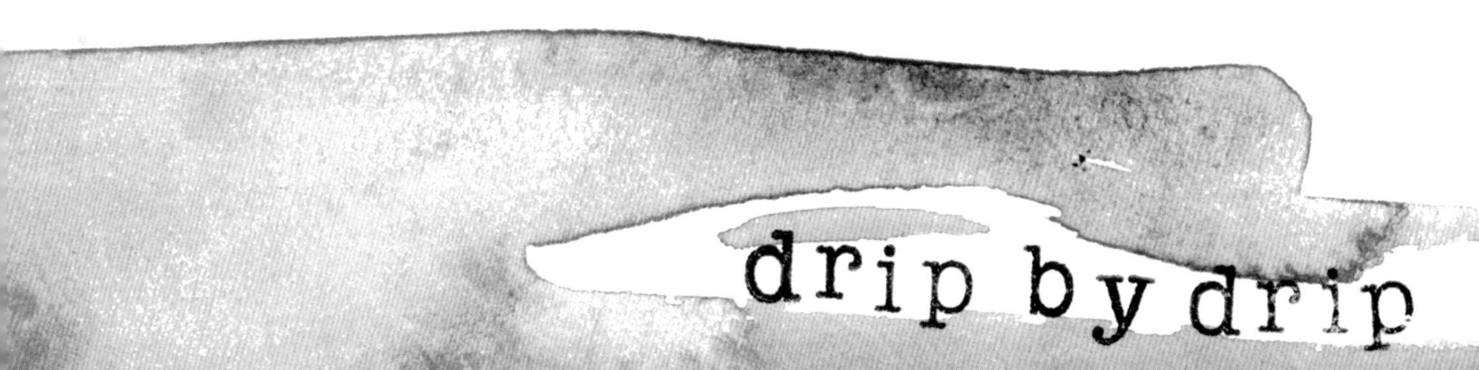

BETWEEN TWO FLOWS:

down-
pour
uprush
over stone and stone and stone

a stillness:

frames

in reflection

spit-
and-wheezing

insatiab

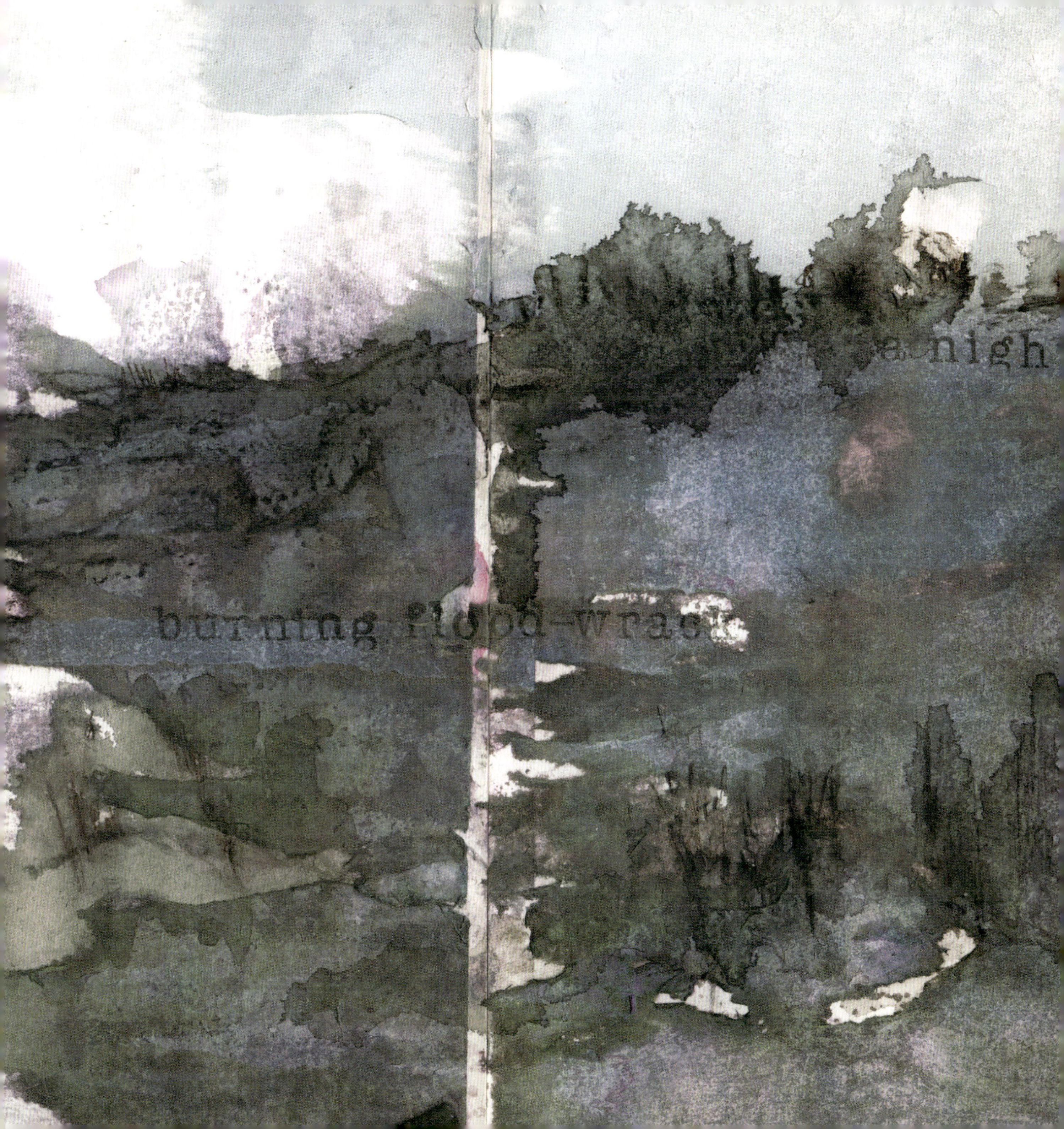
a nigh
burning flood-wrac

flare-up
of fire.
he sky'
small and
bey

each mist-molecule

ye opening on us. See us

maller still, from out there. Space

d amazement. Its unsparing clarity

The Conversation

We could be staring at this flux,
trip and back-rip, this ever-
self-troubling surface
until kingdom come...

till something pocks it, up
from under, where the water
spreads from the pinch

of the bridge, and slows,
and stills; the shadow

makes it visible, a vis-

-itation from its own dimension.
Splash. There. And again.

Fish (or String Theory)
might account for this
irruption of one process

    into, in and through
another... much as this
    rippling shiftless shift
        of interference patterns, con-

    -versation, moves
of itself, without moving, as
    silk flows, its waves

        of moiré, something of
    us and between us, made of

you and me, yet neither me nor you.

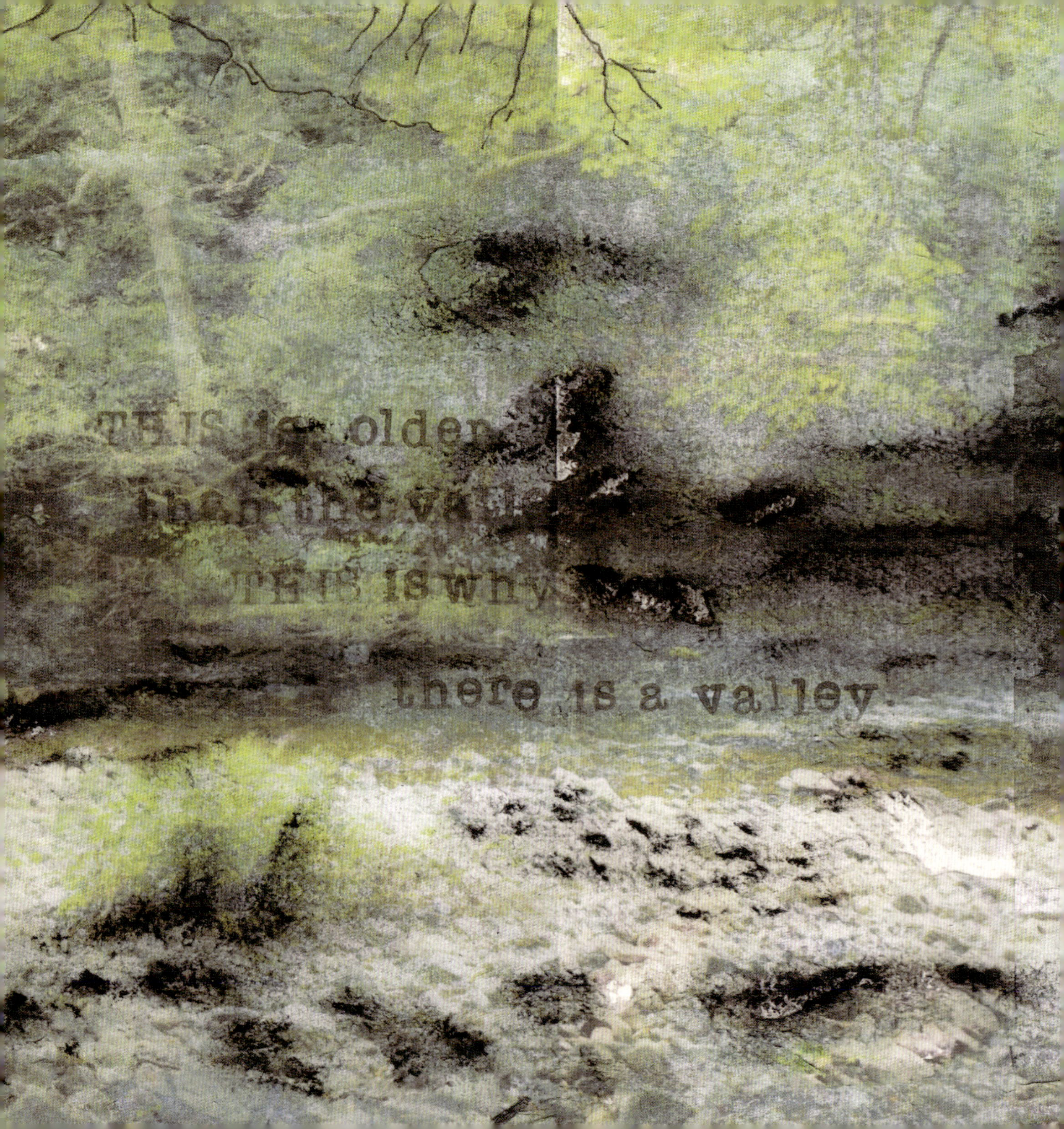
THIS is older
than the vall
THIS is why
there is a valley.

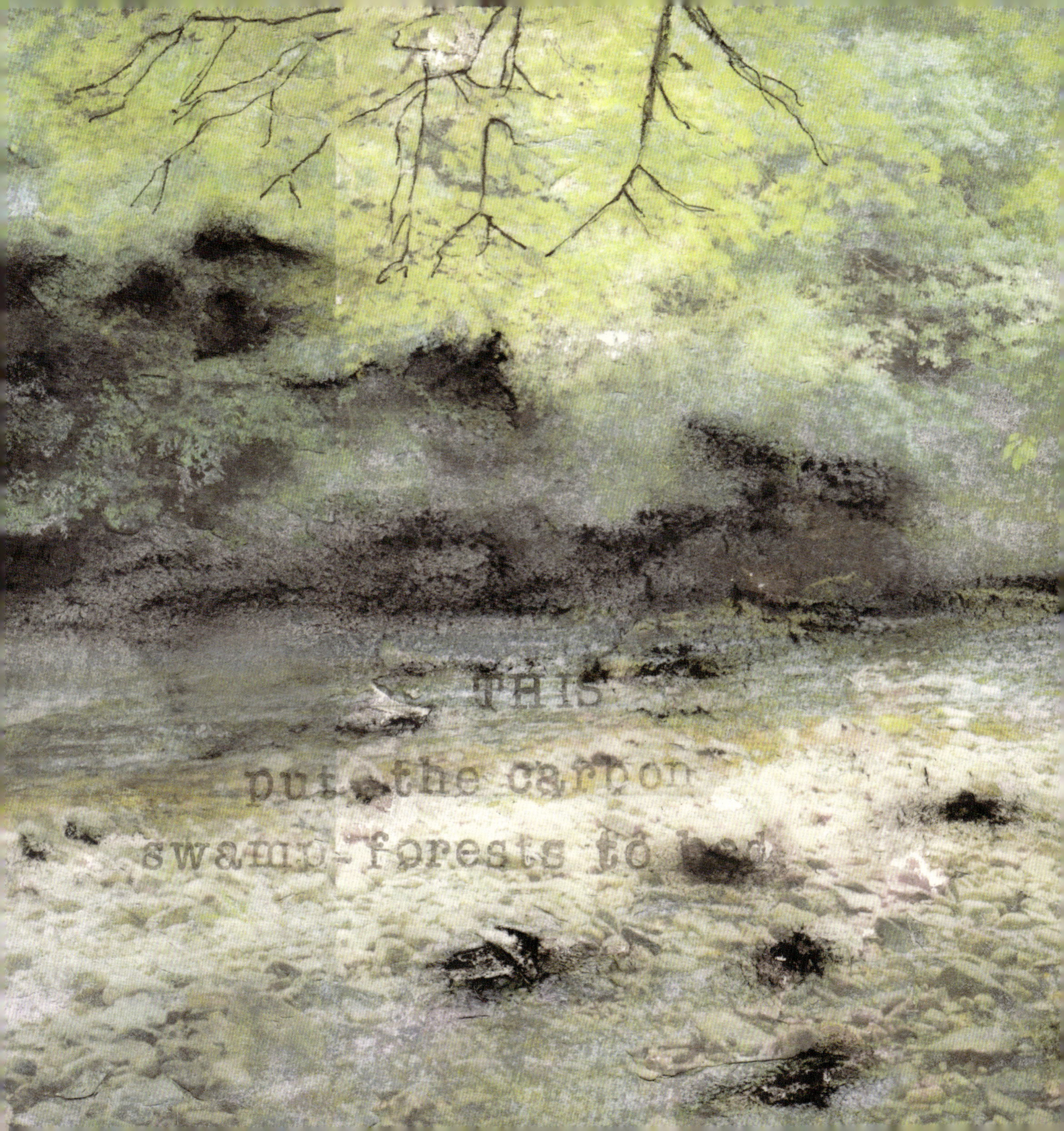
THIS
put the carbon
swamp-forests to bed

The Long Game

It stops me
        between grey slab,
    step and handrail, between
timetabled slots (running late). The sound
of water.
        Sudden. And
    unchanging. It blinks clear
of its conduit, just long enough to wear

our haste, our
        faces, on the blank
    sheet of its white noise,
its audible hush – our world flipped
upside down,
        left / right.
    It seems to know us
inside out. We're in the grip of it –

of gravity,
        which is the will
    of water. This is older
than the valley. This is why there is

a valley. This
put the carbon
swamp-forests to bed
in a black seam like fossilised lightning,

this is what drips
in empty workings,
what leaks from the iron lode,
rust blood... Compared to this, a century
is Basho's
moment: *old*
pond – frog jumps – sound
of water... Still, we have our work: to be

reflections
who reflect
on all that throws them,
who catch at the swerves and feints of how
the water plays
the light, the light
the water; who are in the game
of knowledge (as the manager said: *not*

a matter of life and death...
more important than that.)

Knowing The River

That the Taff is a species of fire
we know:
                over stones,
                                    by its sound,
by its spark, the way it strikes itself

on the flints of them. That this fire
was once a water,
                            mangrove,
                                            mulch
slowed to stone, to a species of sleep

in which king Carbon with his stooping
knights,
            blind horses,
                                fossils, and us,
was laid waiting, in time out of mind.

That the river remembered it, knew it
in its stones,
                    its ink-
                              black blood,

a fact now as gone as... who remembers

carbon ribbons out of which we pecked
words
          with pick-strokes,
                                        pernickity
levers...? That all this we equally know

this summer Sunday as the A470 unreels
its miles,
             the bikers' club,
                                        the stifled
fire of motors, just beyond the trees,

while here the water tells itself
like rolling news,
                          that end
                                        -less footnote
to the future. That the Taff is a species

of knowing. Not one we can have or hold.

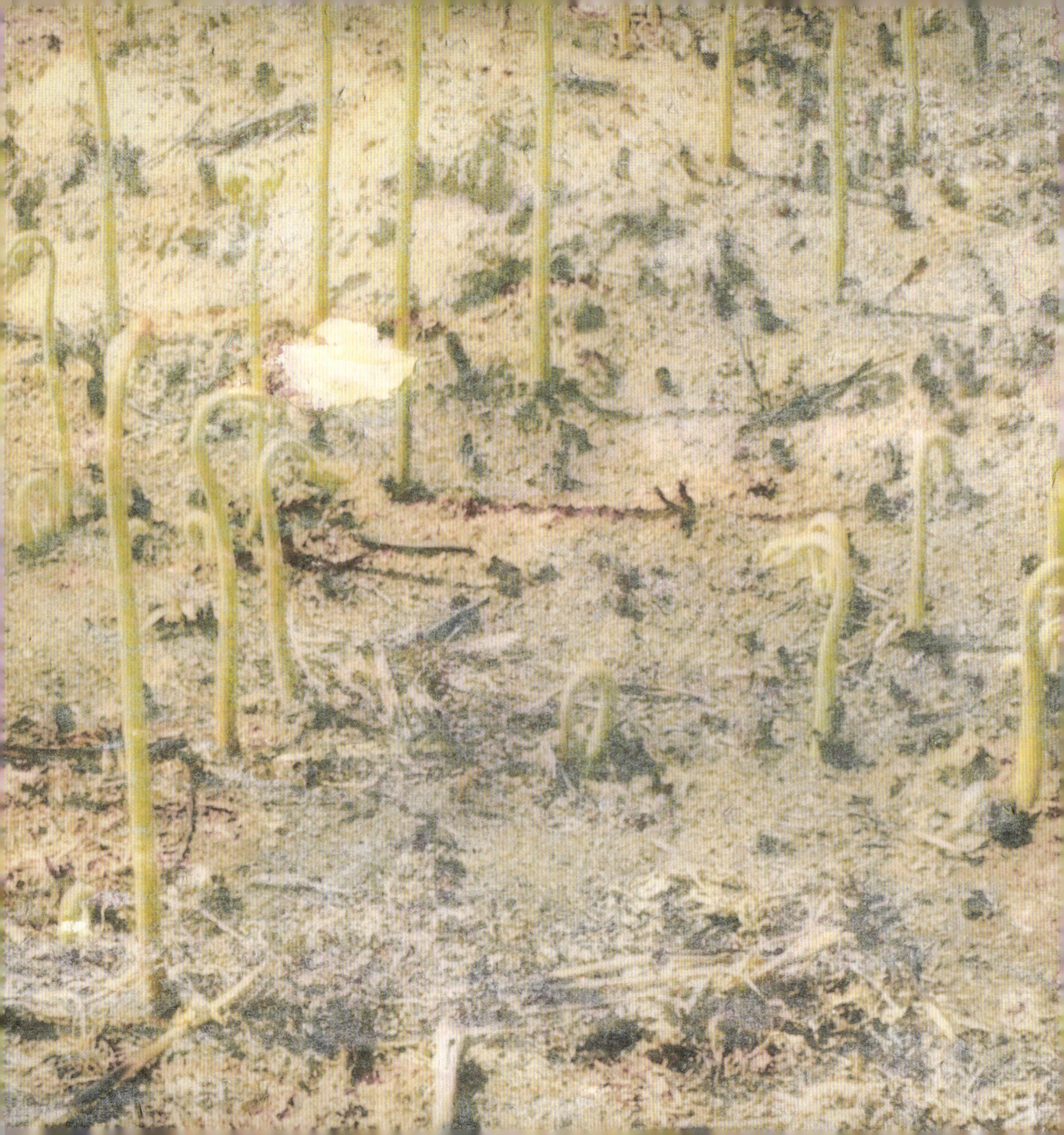

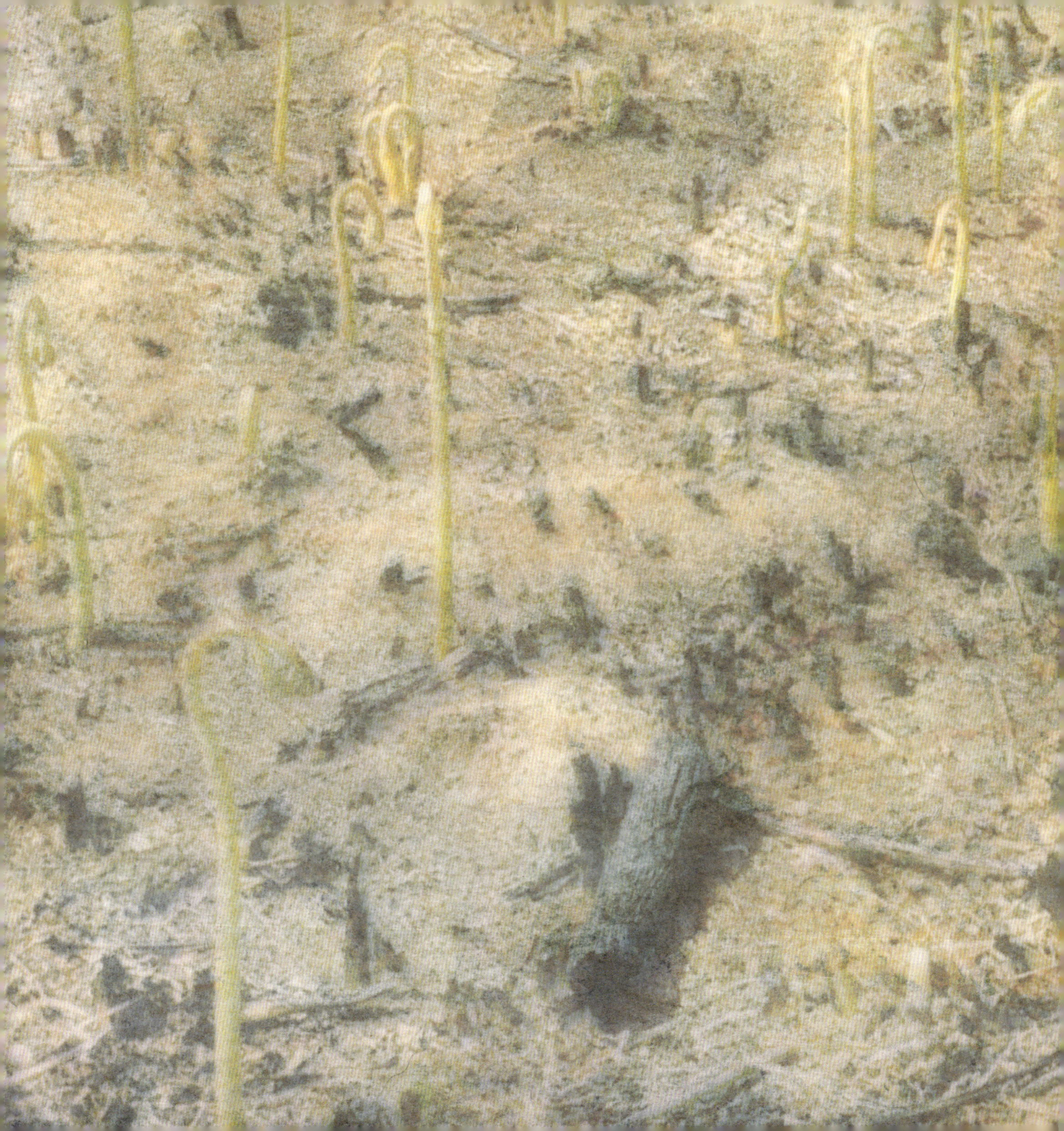

Torched

And here, by the old stone pack-bridge, by the hush
of quick waters, at the track's end (lest
we rhapsodise)
                    is a torched Fiesta,
          blister crusts and sooty freckles
in the scorched paint that's no colour, sea-changed
to coral by fire;

upholstery refined to black talc
in a circuit diagram of fine springs, trims and wires,

rear windscreen popped out whole by the writhe
of buckling steel and the fists of heat pressure inside.

Sunk on its axles, in the mucking-out of its own innards,
almost comfy in its well-fouled nest…
Don't ask why

but how. Just a match
in the tank? Are you nuts? my gentle
neighbour looks at me concerned, as if I'd
had a misspent childhood;

you siphon a gallon, douse a quick
libation then dribble a fuse – oh, and a twist

of rag to give the flame a leg-up, like a courtesy.
Then run like hell. We share a grin. At least, we try.

A revenant of burning rubber, raised, not laid,
by the oncoming rain, stays on
as we go. Two or three
a month, it's regular.
Failed phoenix. But each time it beats
those tattered wings of flame, you'd swear one day
it'll make it to the sky.

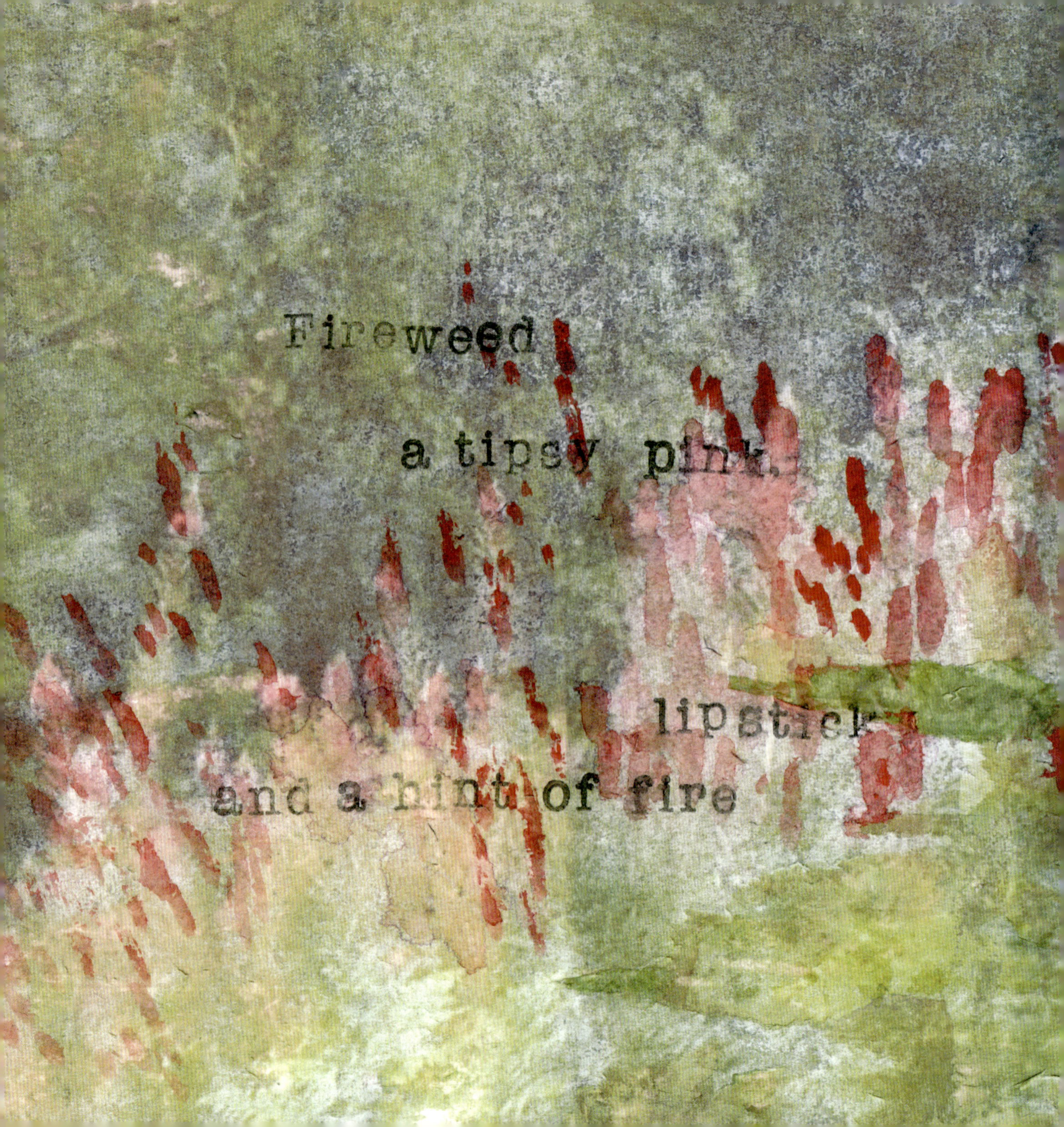
Fireweed
a tipsy pink
lipstick
and a hint of fire

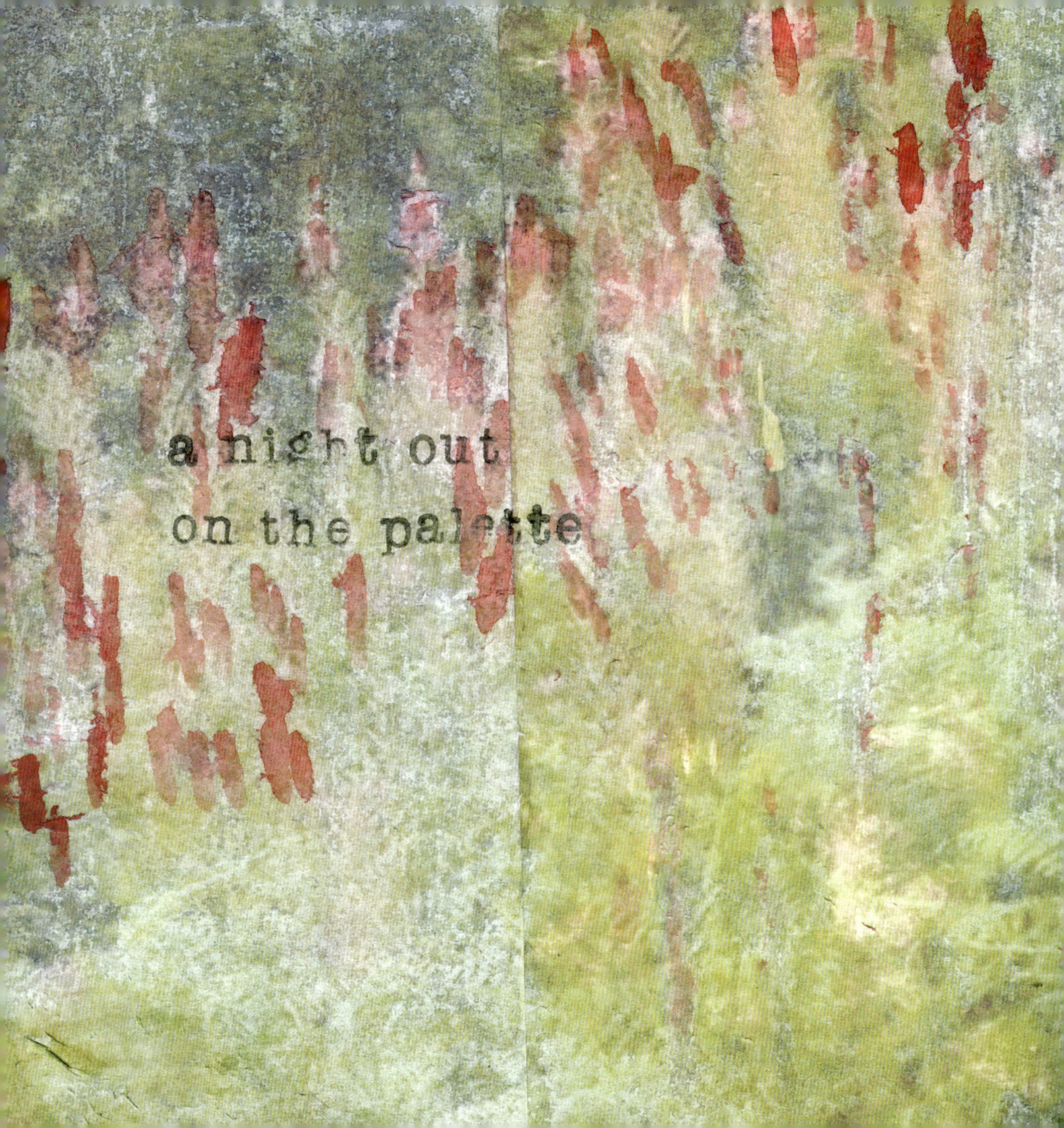
a night out
on the palette

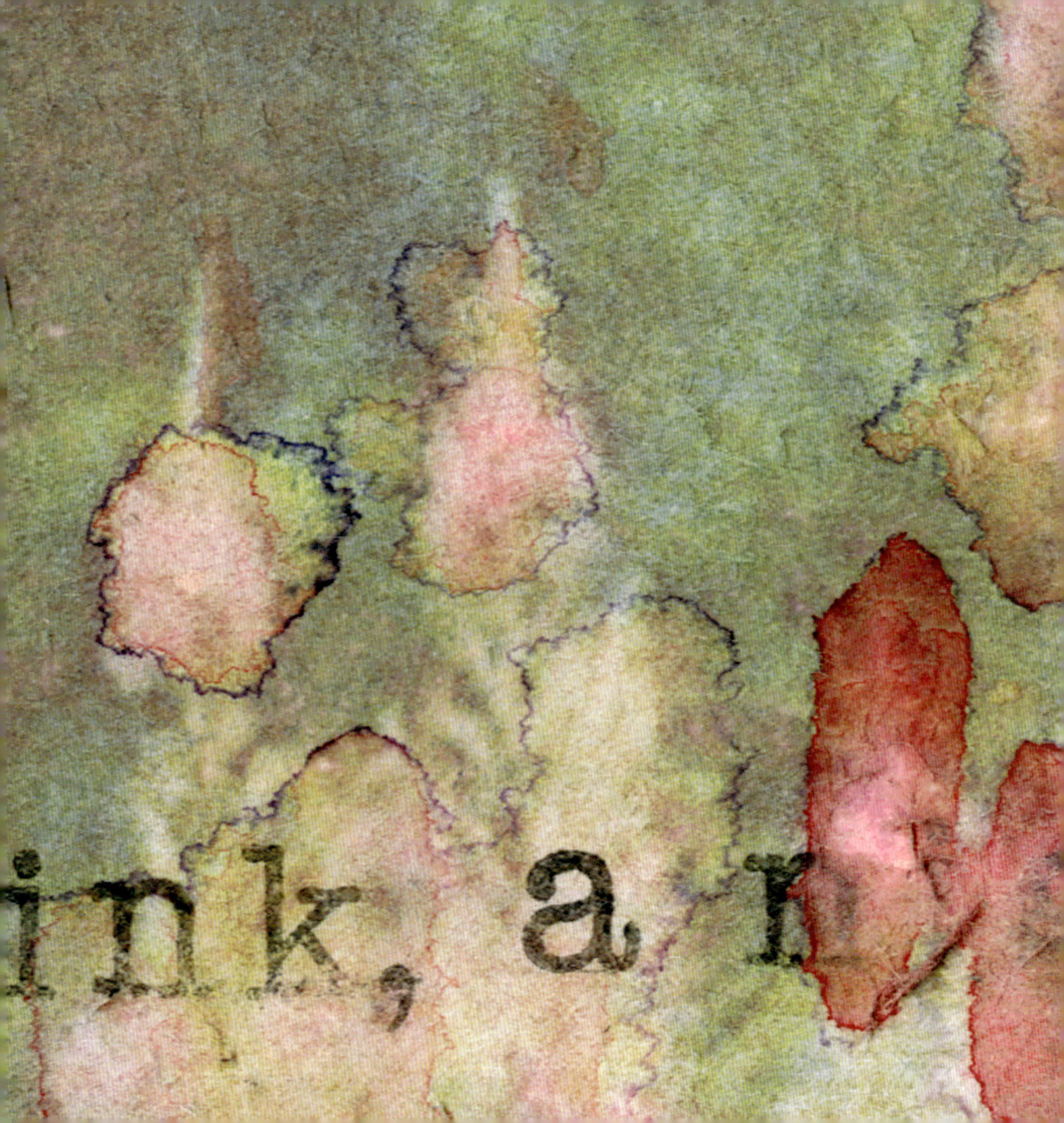
ink, a

Fireweed

a tipsy pink, a night out
on the palette – mixing

Bloody Marys, lipstick,
a hint of the flare-up to come

*

as kids we played on bombsites,
the badlands of railway lines,

untimely places – back then
there was no such thing as waste

*

always first on the scene,
a bit too soon, after disasters

see us in the background
of the newsreel, inappropriately
dressed

*

one day, all this will be wisps
of white, of seed like grown smoke

forgetting ourselves into the future
wildly, willy-nilly, with a will

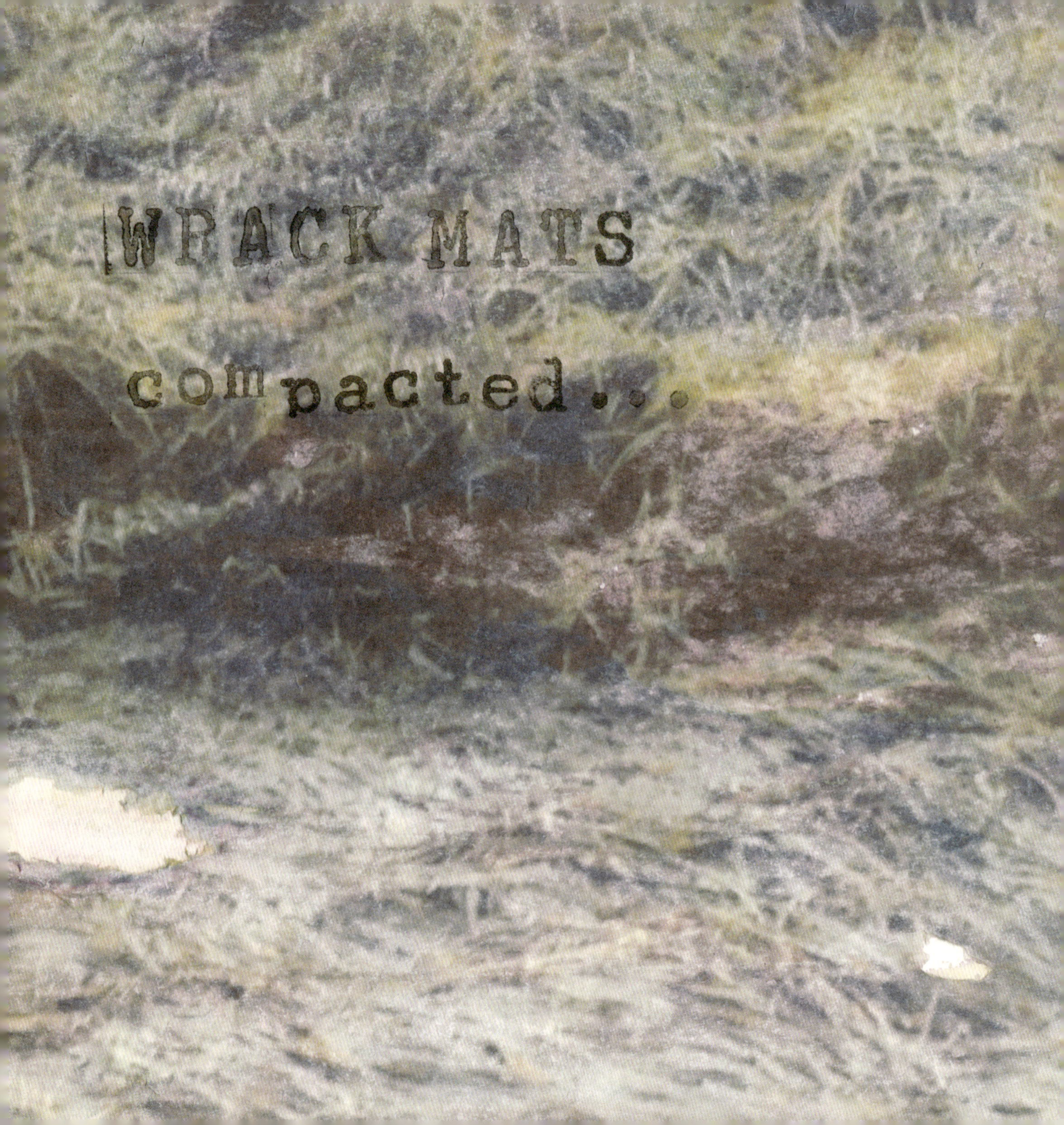

WRACK MATS

compacted...

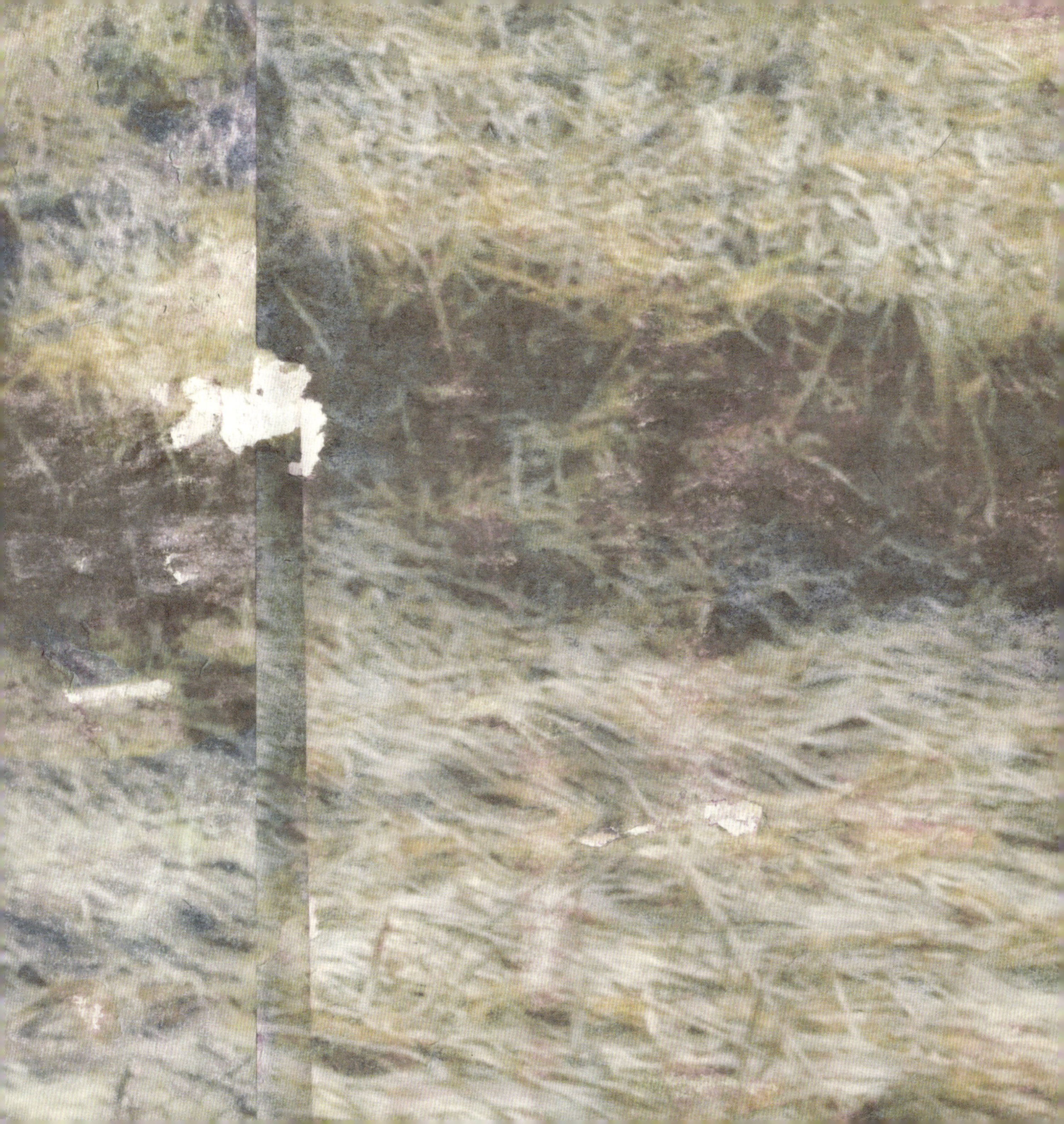

almost woven, like wat

catching everything:

of the floodbird, flo

Packed.

,le. It's a drift net

Or the nest

n for now-

... **WRACK MATS** compacted against this tree or that / yards from the water line – a disconnected / recollection: did it really...? did I dream it...? Packed, // almost woven, like wattle. It's a clogged drain / choking on grass, plastic, / bottles, old lace curtains, condoms, twine.

Sometimes it's the shape of the swirl, the eddy, / the three-times-round something's instinct / made it do before it could sleep. Or the nest // of the floodbird, flown for now – / as twiggily improvised as a swan's or migratory crane's, / defended, in its season, with the same ferocity.

Reeling in the River

Enough now. Wind back the reel;
spool in the river, right up to the source
          which is no one where

unless you hold it cupped
in the all-angled lens of a raindrop – that
or the quivering globe of all this
          for the most part sea.

Scroll up the chattering, brief brilliances
and long abradings, sweeping up of everything

that we let slip, the murk-dynamics
that we might mistake for memory.

          Tease it back
into fine and finer upstreams,
unbraiding its locks, its neat or frayed seams

          unpicked equally.
Wind in its fibres, as if any one might be
the golden fleece, the child's
first clipping in a tarnished locket,

the micron-thin glittering hawser that (why
are we drawn to say this, and so often?)

might *stretch from the earth to the moon.*

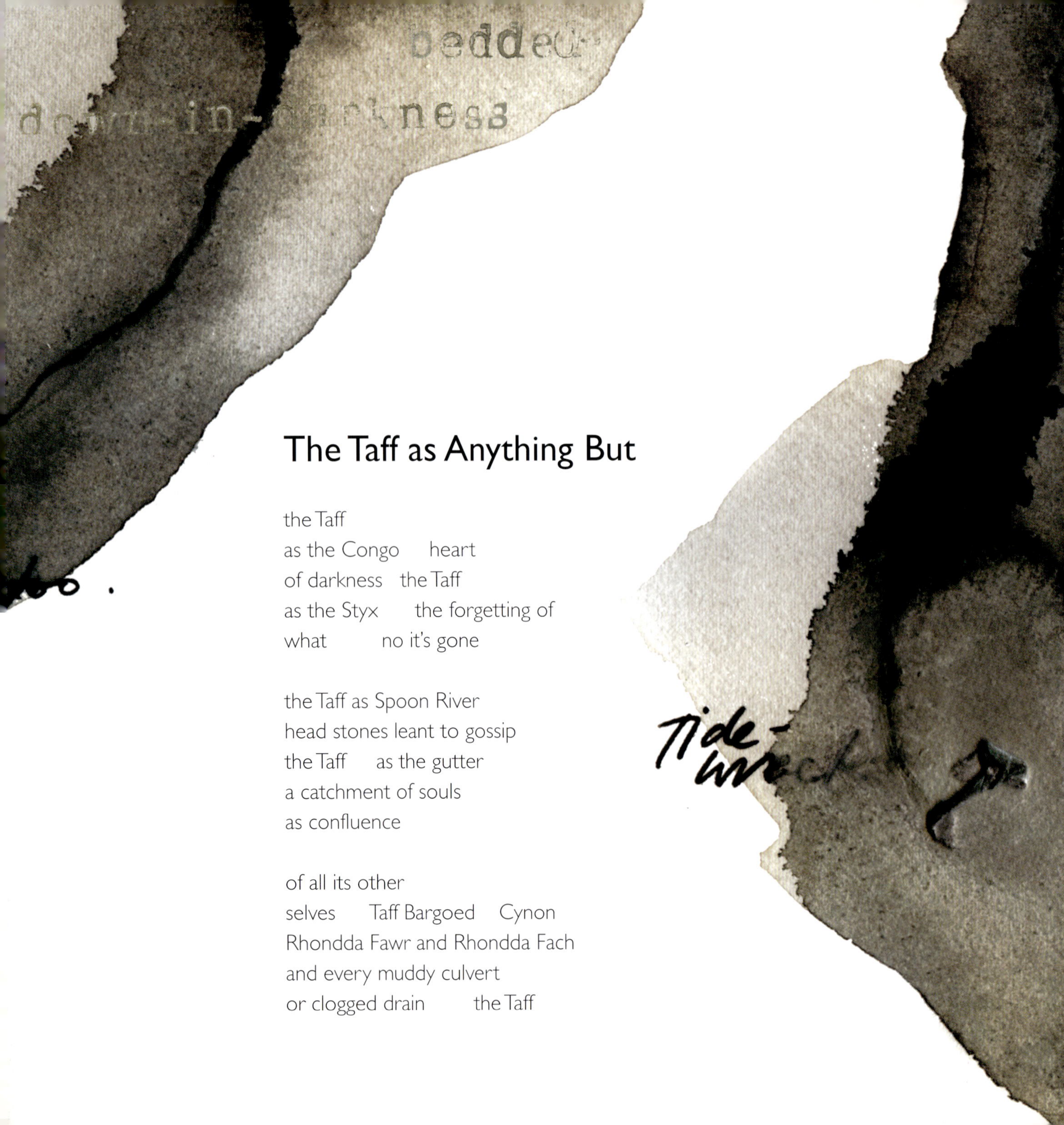

The Taff as Anything But

the Taff
as the Congo   heart
of darkness   the Taff
as the Styx   the forgetting of
what   no it's gone

the Taff as Spoon River
head stones leant to gossip
the Taff   as the gutter
a catchment of souls
as confluence

of all its other
selves   Taff Bargoed   Cynon
Rhondda Fawr and Rhondda Fach
and every muddy culvert
or clogged drain   the Taff

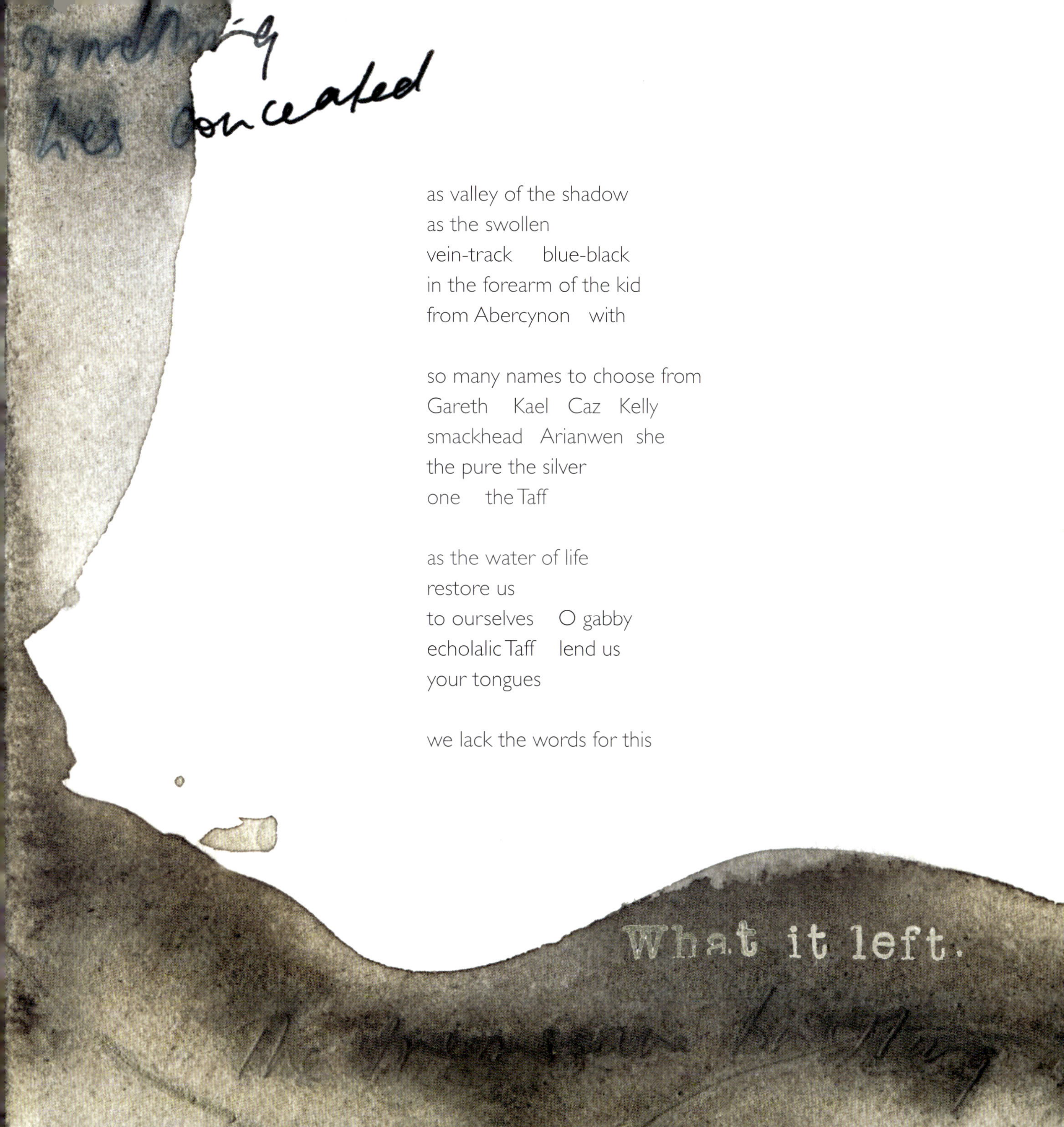

as valley of the shadow
as the swollen
vein-track   blue-black
in the forearm of the kid
from Abercynon   with

so many names to choose from
Gareth   Kael   Caz   Kelly
smackhead   Arianwen   she
the pure the silver
one   the Taff

as the water of life
restore us
to ourselves   O gabby
echolalic Taff   lend us
your tongues

we lack the words for this

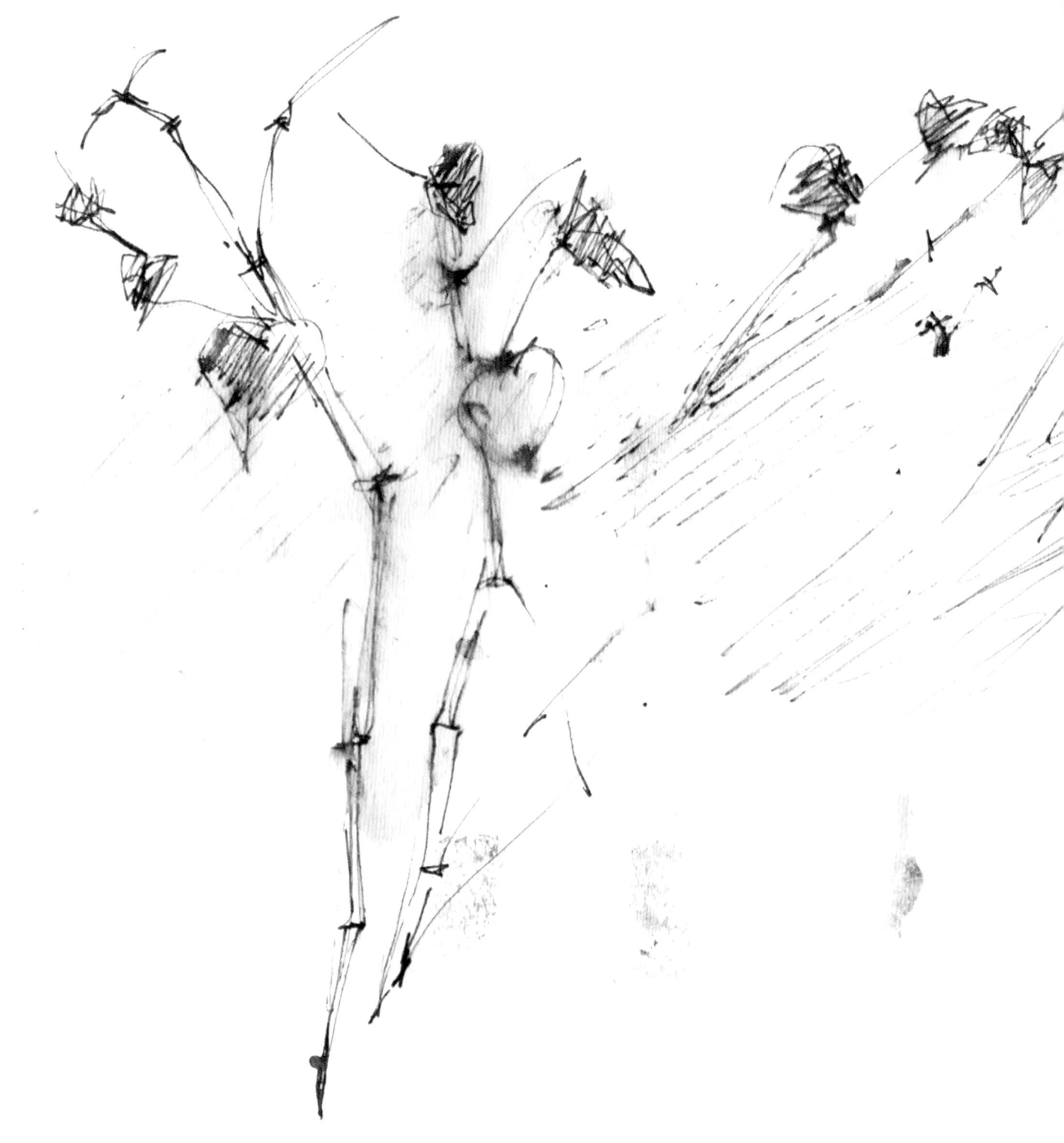

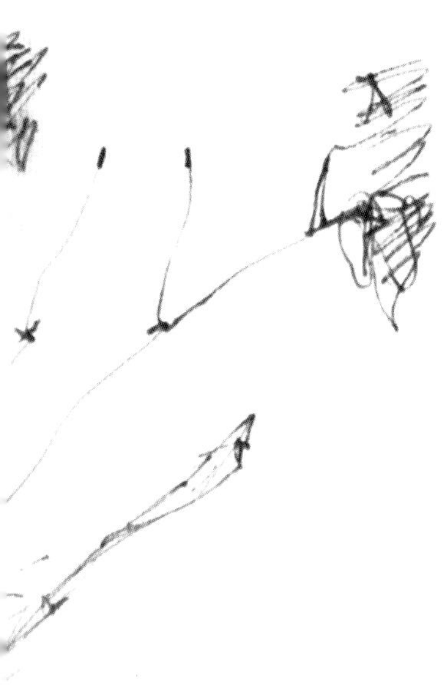

… BAG TATTERS:

twig-snagged,
or in crooks of stumbled trees
as tough as an old grudge
won't loose their grip but rip to streamers
featherings like (spread-
eagled in the tidewrack) a drowned gull's
once white or once transparent
they converge to glaucous grey
one hangs in a hunch
above the shallows like a heron's watchfulness
sans bird, or there, implausibly
high in a tree, another flaps in the wind
the flight of one
wing flapping, as the Zen monk did not say

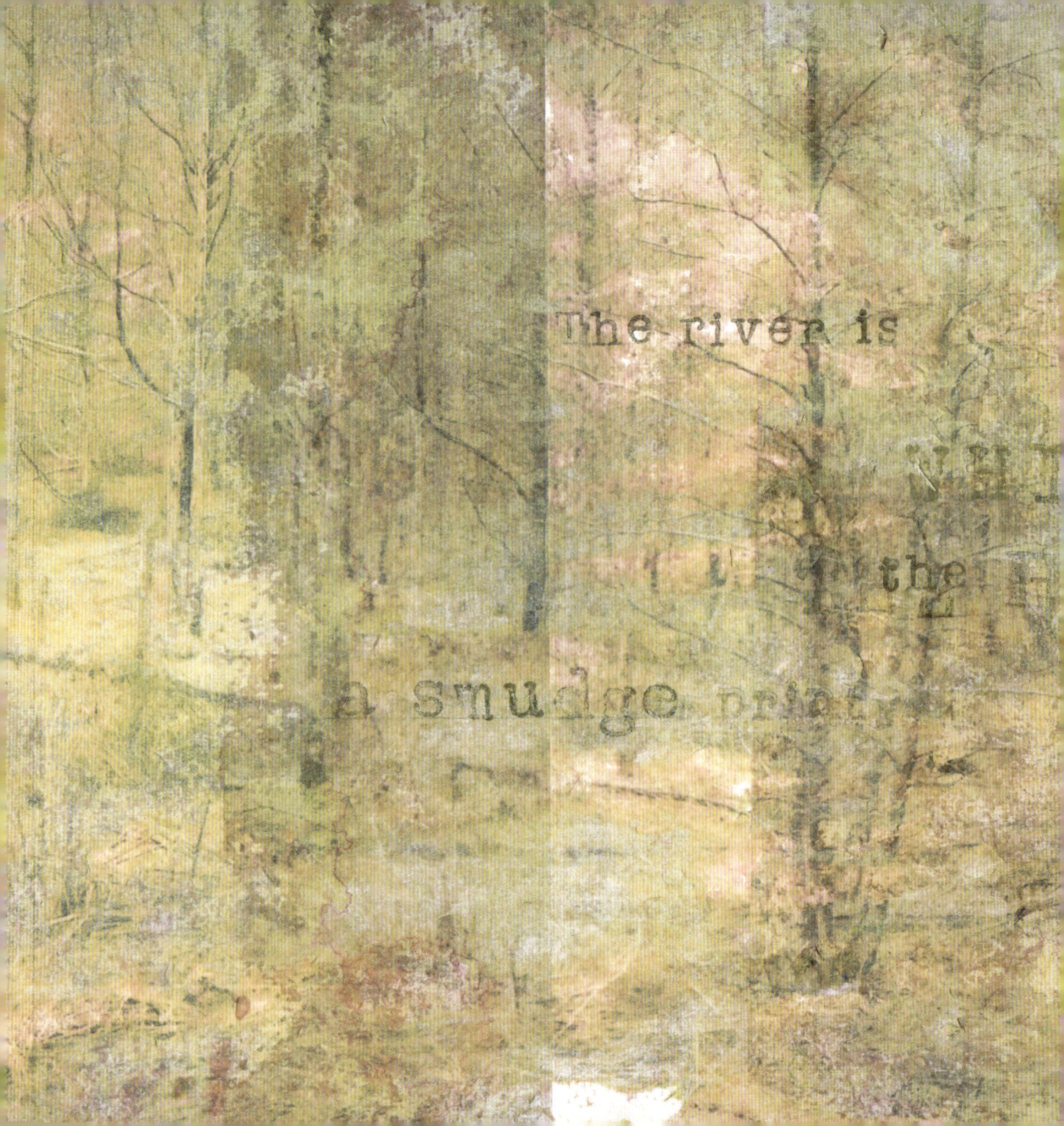
The river is
the
a smudge print

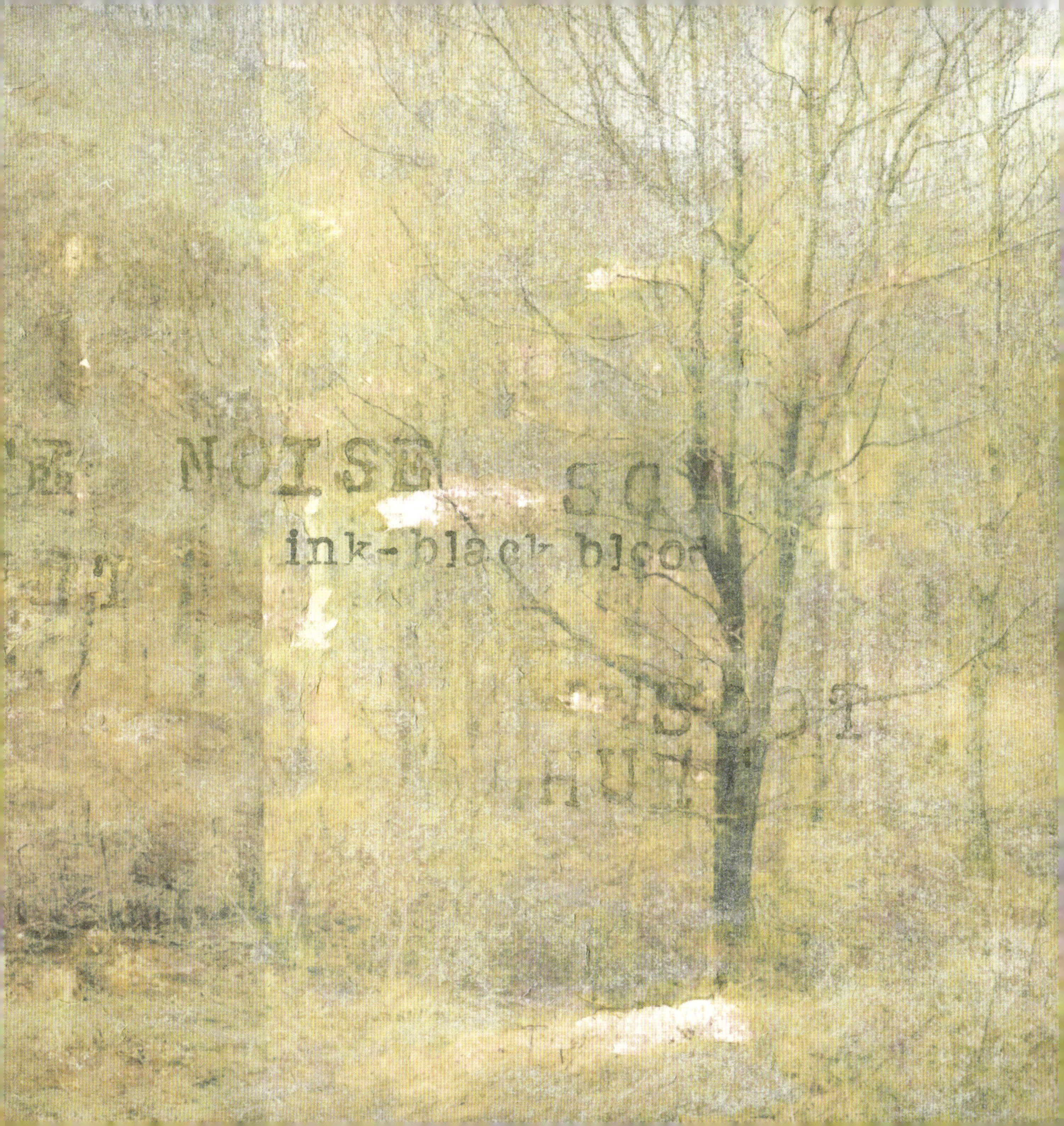
NOISE
ink-black

Sketching the Taff in Charcoal

Before the furnace had them

and before the bared flanks (bracken
like a gutted mattress, all its wires and springs)...

Before the charcoal and before the black muck-rock
came up out of prehistory, out of bedded-
down-in-darkness forests of its own...

Before the smoulder bearing news
there would be fire to come, and a future

that branched into tunnels, and the blast and the hack of it,

and then the silence, hush like a down-tools walkout,
hush like the first moment after the thud,

more felt than heard, that no one knew yet
had been it, the explosion – hush into which
you step out, a century later, workless, un-manned...

Before all this, there were trees
and the wind in their leaves,

tongues, each an utterance

as indeterminate as smoke is, as the river's
wish-rush, or the new-same wind now

through the new trees. Render this
in charcoal. Sketch us in another future
now the one we thought we had is past and gone.

The mountain of dross which had startled me on the preceding night with its terrific glare, looked now nothing more than an immense dark heap of cinders. It is only when the shades of night have settled down that the fire within manifests itself, making the hill appear an immense glowing mass. (George Borrow, 1862)

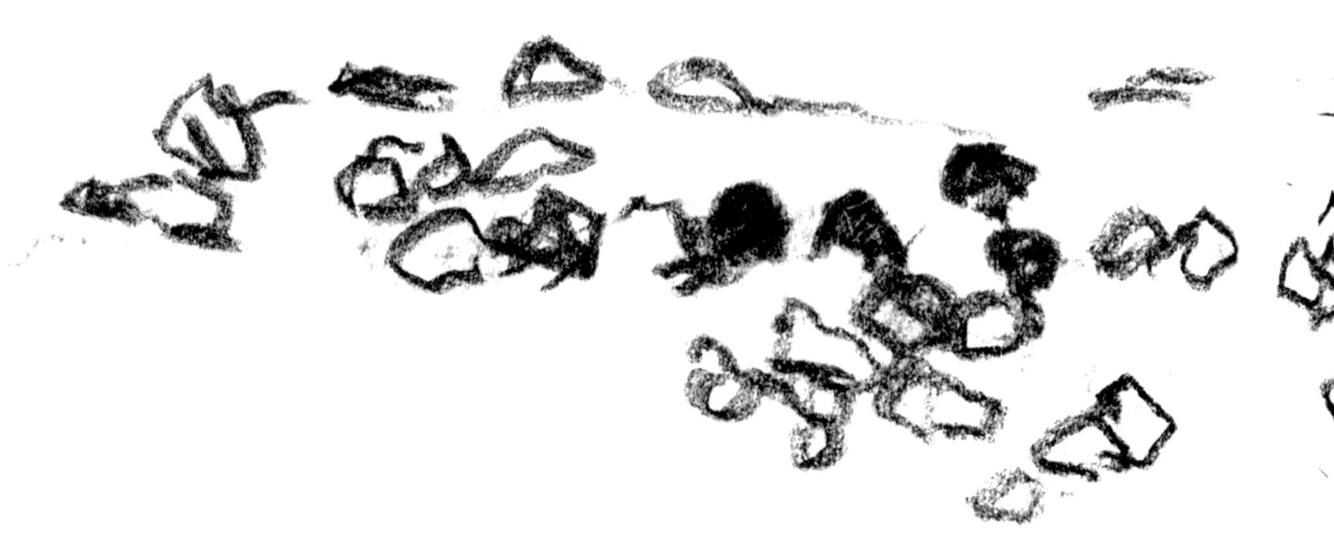

… **NO MATTER HOW** the rain goes on, or the river
repeats just to carry away,
this stays

grained in the creases,
vowels that drop and dwell,
then the lift:

the voice. Change the words as we may,
the Valleys won't wash out,

there like a watermark in water,
something the rain itself might say.

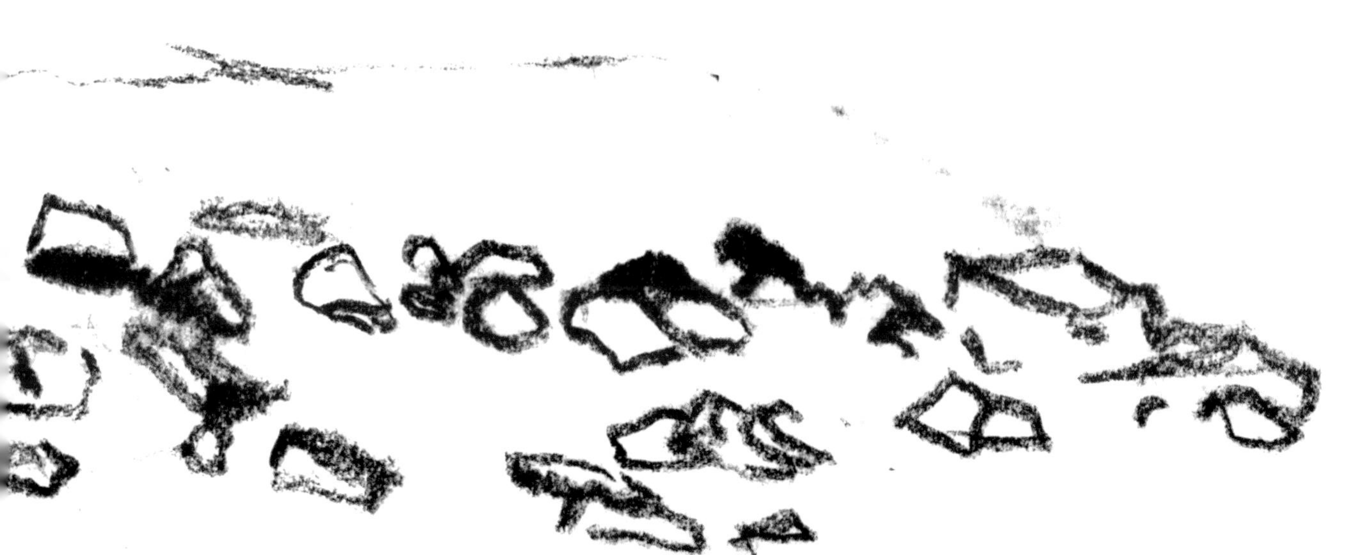

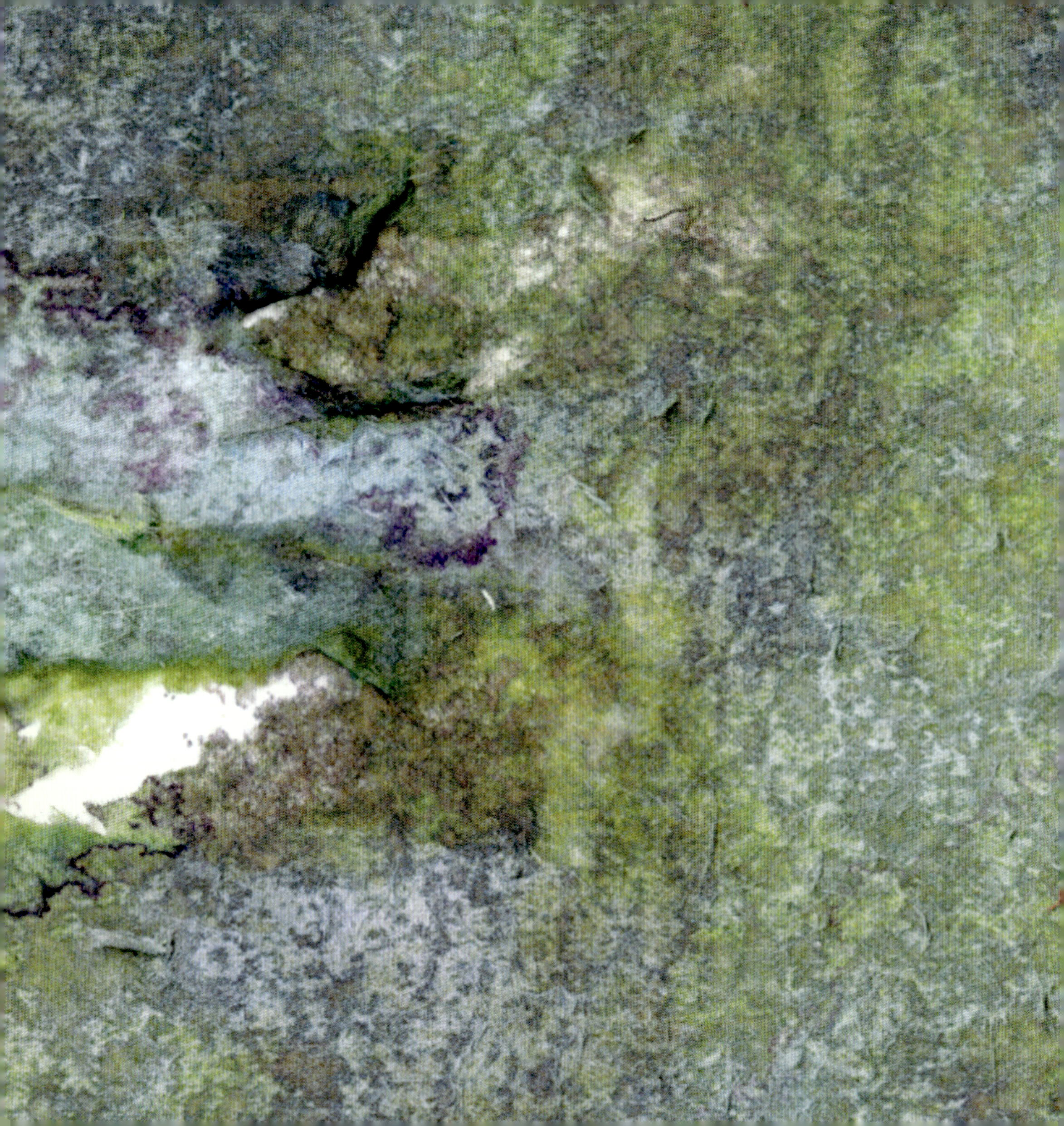

Praise Song for the Taff

Start
by mistrusting the beauty
of this hillside,
smoother than it should be,
green as a hospital sheet,

stretched up tight to his jutting stony chin,

the laid-out giant,
grand old bugger –
half ogre, half rough-you-up-
and-make-a-man-of-you
tough uncle. Don't let them trim quite all

the stubble, not quite sluice away

the phlegm
stained black.
Find someone, if
there's anyone, to belt out
something rousing for him

as he belted all and sundry in his day.

And then
mistrust the river,
its apparent clarities.

The fish have come back
alive-alive-O with tidings
that something has died.

And a kingfisher,
welding-torch blue.

The water, though, twinkles
with forgetfulness
of how the coal dust flowed

rimming the stone-beach
and the flood marks under bridges

right down to the bay, the swish
of its shitty and muscular tail
for miles into the Bristol Channel.

Mistrust the sigh
                                        of emptiness. The quiet.
The unbroached skyline. Because anytime now

there'll be the buzz-saw snarl of petty biking,
their scars on the hillside. Here's a posse, shiftily
of several ages, round a torched tree stump

on the waste ground which is also
beautiful,

with gorse and slim tentative birch trunks
and fat blackberries
by the *Do Not Cross The Railway* sign,

with its *Danger of Death*, a well-
worn path up to and from it either side.

And last,
mistrust mistrust,
the need to be unfooled, uncompromised

as if any water you could drink
was pure and might not rise

against us, against toppled boughs
dammed under bridges, and its own back-swelling.

Nowhere anyone can stand is high and dry.

Mistrust all that, and yourself, and now,
consider
just the possibility

of praise.

START

by mistrusting the beauty

AND THEN

MISTRUST THE SIGH

mistrust the river,

of emptiness. The quiet.

AND LAST

mistrust mistrust

... **WHY SHOULD YOU EXPECT** it to smile for you, this river? Grow up. New rains, a half-metre rise, the Taff is murky, greenish-grey and tetchy – a sour smell too, slightly chemical, slightly tinged with mould. It's an unlovely river today, the last leaves falling, everything as naked as you've seen it. That's *naked*, not *nude* – there's nothing posed about it, or alluring, in its least-best angle, with its uncleared rubbish too. Unlovely, it doesn't say *Love me*. Yet you do.

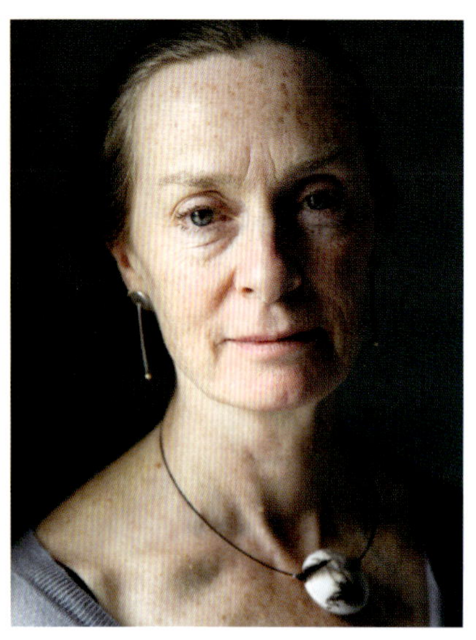

Valerie Coffin Price is a Welsh artist-letterer living and working in Cardiff, who grew up in the Welsh Marches and Singapore. She trained in Fine Art at Chelsea School of Art and the City & Guilds of London Art School, as well as training as a dancer in America. She has exhibited extensively both nationally and internationally, including the Hayward Gallery, London; Douglas Hyde Gallery, Dublin; Pitt Rivers Museum, Oxford; Centre des Migrations, Québec and the Natural History Museum in London. Recent solo exhibitions include The River Next Door (2015), Intimate Cartographies(2011), Distant Voices (2007) and Territoires (2003). Valerie comes from a long line of military and colonial travellers and has continued in their footsteps with her work responding to wild and remote landscapes, which has taken her as far afield as Russia (1990), Québec (1998, 2002, 2003) and Cambodia (2005), but always comes back to a close and intimate relationship to river and border landscapes in Wales and along the English border.

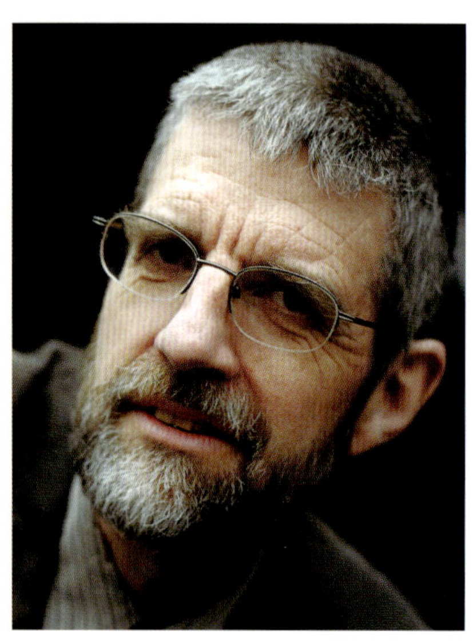

Philip Gross was born beside the slate quarry of Delabole, North Cornwall, and grew up in Plymouth. His father's experience as a wartime refugee from Estonia informs much of his work. He studied English at Sussex University and survived as a freelance writer, visiting schools and teaching writing classes, before coming to work in universities. Since 2004 he has been been Professor of Creative Writing at Glamorgan University (now University of South Wales). He lives in Penarth. In 1982 he won the National Poetry Competition with the title poem of his first collection The Ice Factory, and since then has published nearly twenty collections, most recently Deep Field (2011) and Later (2013). He has collaborated with artists, musicians, dancers and puppeteers. The Water Table won the T.S.Eliot Prize in 2009, I Spy Pinhole Eye, with photographer Simon Denison, won Wales Book of The Year 2010, and Off Road to Everywhere won the CLPE Award for Children's Poetry 2011.